9/18/12 $5.95   70.01 3ER

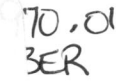

STERLING

Christopher Columbus

The Voyage that Changed the World

Emma Carlson Berne

PROPERTY OF DEL NORTE MIDDLE SCHOOL DEL NORTE, CO 81132

STERLING

New York / London
www.sterlingpublishing.com/kids

For Aaron

STERLING and the distinctive Sterling logo are registered trademarks of
Sterling Publishing Co., Inc.

Library of Congress Cataloging-in-Publication Data

Berne, Emma Carlson.
  Christopher Columbus : the voyage that changed the world / by Emma Carlson Bernay.
    p. cm. — (Sterling biographies)
  Includes bibliographical references and index.
  ISBN-13: 978-1-4027-4407-5
  ISBN-10: 1-4027-4407-2
  1. Columbus, Christopher—Juvenile literature. 2. Explorers—America—Biography—Juvenile
literature. 3. Explorers—Spain—Biography—Juvenile literature. 4. America—Discovery and
exploration—Spanish—Juvenile literature. I. Title.

E111.B53 2008
970.01'5092—dc22
[B]
                                          2007048197
Lot#:
10 9 8 7 6 5 4 3 2
01/10

Published by Sterling Publishing Co., Inc.
387 Park Avenue South, New York, NY 10016
© 2008 by Emma Carlson Berne
Distributed in Canada by Sterling Publishing
c/o Canadian Manda Group, 165 Dufferin Street
Toronto, Ontario, Canada M6K 3H6
Distributed in the United Kingdom by GMC Distribution Services
Castle Place, 166 High Street, Lewes, East Sussex, England BN7 1XU
Distributed in Australia by Capricorn Link (Australia) Pty. Ltd.
P.O. Box 704, Windsor, NSW 2756, Australia

Printed in China
All rights reserved

Sterling ISBN 978-1-4027-4407-5 (paperback)
        ISBN 978-1-4027-6056-3 (hardcover)

For information about custom editions, special sales, premium and
corporate purchases, please contact Sterling Special Sales
Department at 800-805-5489 or specialsales@sterlingpublishing.com.

Designed for SimonSays Design! by Frieda Christofides
Image research by Carolyn Chappo and Susan Schader

Contents

Events in the Life of Christopher Columbus

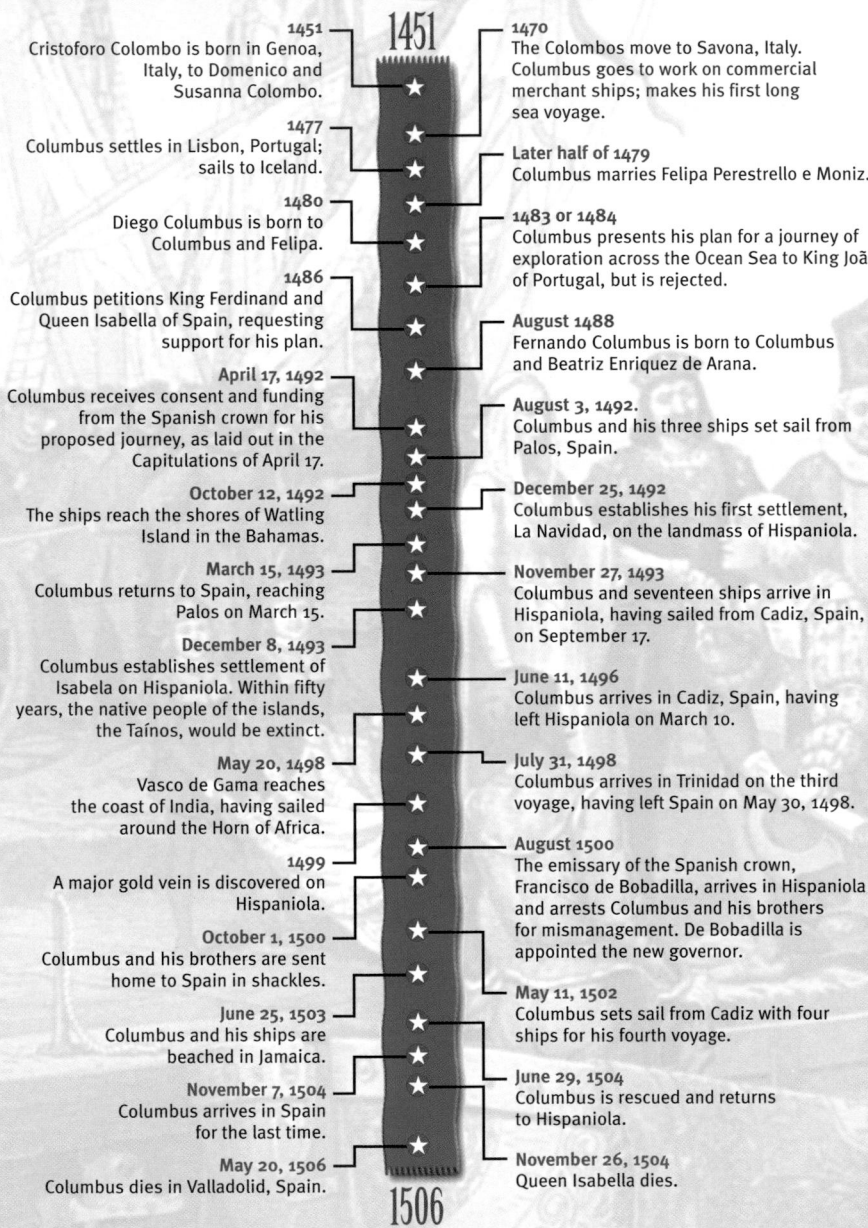

1451
Cristoforo Colombo is born in Genoa, Italy, to Domenico and Susanna Colombo.

1477
Columbus settles in Lisbon, Portugal; sails to Iceland.

1480
Diego Columbus is born to Columbus and Felipa.

1486
Columbus petitions King Ferdinand and Queen Isabella of Spain, requesting support for his plan.

April 17, 1492
Columbus receives consent and funding from the Spanish crown for his proposed journey, as laid out in the Capitulations of April 17.

October 12, 1492
The ships reach the shores of Watling Island in the Bahamas.

March 15, 1493
Columbus returns to Spain, reaching Palos on March 15.

December 8, 1493
Columbus establishes settlement of Isabela on Hispaniola. Within fifty years, the native people of the islands, the Taínos, would be extinct.

May 20, 1498
Vasco de Gama reaches the coast of India, having sailed around the Horn of Africa.

1499
A major gold vein is discovered on Hispaniola.

October 1, 1500
Columbus and his brothers are sent home to Spain in shackles.

June 25, 1503
Columbus and his ships are beached in Jamaica.

November 7, 1504
Columbus arrives in Spain for the last time.

May 20, 1506
Columbus dies in Valladolid, Spain.

1451

1470
The Colombos move to Savona, Italy. Columbus goes to work on commercial merchant ships; makes his first long sea voyage.

Later half of 1479
Columbus marries Felipa Perestrello e Moniz.

1483 or 1484
Columbus presents his plan for a journey of exploration across the Ocean Sea to King João of Portugal, but is rejected.

August 1488
Fernando Columbus is born to Columbus and Beatriz Enriquez de Arana.

August 3, 1492.
Columbus and his three ships set sail from Palos, Spain.

December 25, 1492
Columbus establishes his first settlement, La Navidad, on the landmass of Hispaniola.

November 27, 1493
Columbus and seventeen ships arrive in Hispaniola, having sailed from Cadiz, Spain, on September 17.

June 11, 1496
Columbus arrives in Cadiz, Spain, having left Hispaniola on March 10.

July 31, 1498
Columbus arrives in Trinidad on the third voyage, having left Spain on May 30, 1498.

August 1500
The emissary of the Spanish crown, Francisco de Bobadilla, arrives in Hispaniola and arrests Columbus and his brothers for mismanagement. De Bobadilla is appointed the new governor.

May 11, 1502
Columbus sets sail from Cadiz with four ships for his fourth voyage.

June 29, 1504
Columbus is rescued and returns to Hispaniola.

November 26, 1504
Queen Isabella dies.

1506

A Historic Voyage

The Admiral most seriously urged them to keep a
good lookout . . . and to watch carefully for land.

—Bartolome de las Casas

The sun was hot. It blazed whitely overhead, baking the decks of the massive wooden ships. The sailors, sunburned brown and red, wiped the sweat that trickled down their necks as they wrestled the heavy ropes of the **rigging**. The only sounds were the slapping of the waves against the ships' hulls and the constant creaking of wood and iron as the vessels slowly made their way westward.

Christopher Columbus, his crew, and his three ships had been sailing for five weeks. Day after day, the empty waters surrounded them. Day after day, Columbus insisted that they would soon reach their promised land: the Indies. But the journey had gone on too long.

Once again, night fell and the moon rose, its bright path glittering across the water. It was hours past midnight as the sleepy-headed lookout scanned the horizon. Then, his eyes widened. Was it? Could it be?

Yes. There it was—land! Columbus had done it: He was the first man to reach the East by sailing west.

Little did Columbus know or could have imagined that when he sailed across the Atlantic Ocean, he changed the course of human history. He introduced two sides of the world to each other, with consequences both fantastic and devastating. For better or for worse, after 1492, the world would never be the same.

CHAPTER 1

The Boy Cristoforo

Two things which are important to know about every famous man are his birthplace and his family.
—Fernando Columbus

In the year 1451, Genoa, Italy, was a bustling port city, surrounded by massive stone walls and swarming with merchants, sailors, shipbuilders, and craftspeople. From the vast harbor, ships left every day laden with wool, grain, and olive oil. They returned bearing salt, cork, and furs from as far north as Iceland and as far south as the coast of Africa.

The streets of **medieval** Italy were lively and chaotic. There were no sidewalks or street signs—shoppers, vendors, men on horseback, carriages, and livestock all jostled each other in a colorful mix. Giant wooden ships

During the time of Columbus, the docks of Genoa were busy and hectic. The same docks can be seen in the background of this 1856 illustration.

with billowing white sails were anchored in the harbor near the docks. Ropes were strung from their masts and thousands of barnacles and mussels crusted the sides of the ship below the water line. On the shore, men shouted and pointed as bundles were loaded onto carts and wagons. Sailors in their red woolen caps climbed the rigging of the ships or hoisted loads onto their shoulders in preparation for the next journey.

The docks were the heart of trade and commerce in the city. One day, a young man would stand on those docks and think of the big, big dream he had conceived. He would watch the ships sailing out and in his mind's eye, he would see his own ship disappearing over the horizon, himself off for the greatest adventure of his life.

A Middle-Class Family

That young man was Cristoforo Colombo. We know him as Christopher Columbus. He was born in a little house near the eastern gate of Genoa's walls. His father was a wool-weaver named Domenico. His mother was named Susanna, and baby Christopher was her first child. She and Domenico would go on to have four more children, but only three of them would live to adulthood: Bartolomeo, Bianchinetta, and Giacomo, who was called Diego.

The Colombos had always been wool-weavers. It was common during the Middle Ages for families to pass down the same trade for generations. Domenico and his father were no exception. Giovanni Colombo, Christopher's grandfather, was from the little village of Moconesi, about twenty miles east of Genoa. When Domenico was about eleven years old, his father apprenticed him to a local weaver so he could follow in the family business.

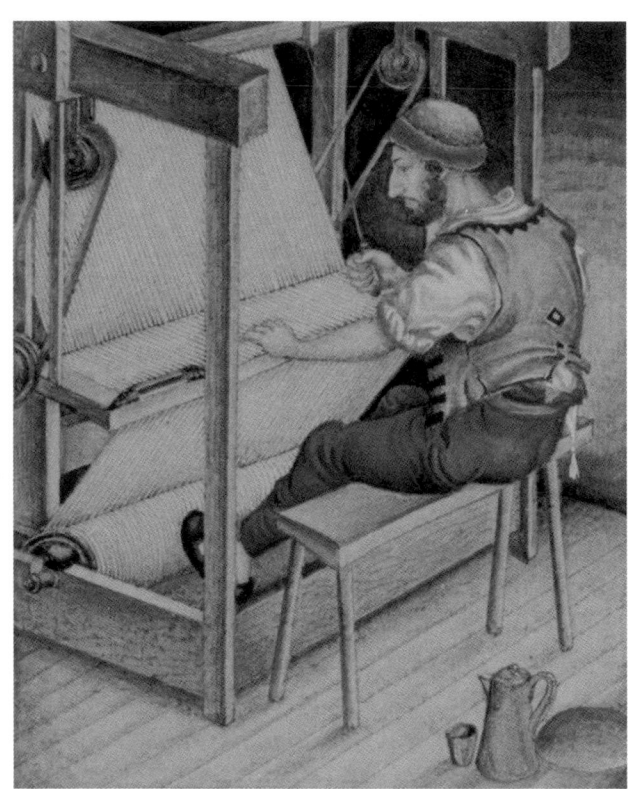

A painting from the Middle Ages depicts a weaver working at his loom, much as Domenico Columbo would have done once he had completed his apprenticeship.

Apprenticeships were a normal part of life in the Middle Ages. Young boys or teenagers whose families wanted them to learn a certain craft were sent to live and work with older, experienced craftsmen called masters. Once the apprentice had mastered the needed skills, he was promoted to the level of journeyman. As a journeyman, he could work on his own pieces, under the supervision of a master. After the production of one final piece—his masterpiece—a journeyman was allowed to become a master.

The Middle Ages

In European history, the years from 500 CE until about 1500 CE are usually defined as the Middle Ages. These years are also referred to as medieval times. The Middle Ages were a period of great political, social, and economic change in Europe. The modern boundaries of Europe's countries were set during this time. In addition, during the Middle Ages, knights rode to Jerusalem in the **Crusades**, and one-third of the entire population of Europe died of a form of plague during the Black Death.

The Pope speaks to nobility in this 1486 painting, encouraging them to join in a Crusade to the holy city of Jerusalem.

Domenico became a master weaver in 1440. After he had reached this level, he was permitted to become a member of the local guild, as all masters were. A guild is an association of craftsmen in one field, and Domenico joined the weavers' guild. Guilds were very important and powerful groups in medieval life: They set the prices for their goods, controlled trade, and dictated the standards each guild member was responsible for upholding. Members belonged to the guild for life, and they were expected to keep the secrets of the guild's particular craft.

Domenico rented the little house near the eastern gate of Genoa and was given the job of gatekeeper. In 1445, he married a girl named Susanna Fontanarossa who was also the daughter of a weaver. Almost nothing is known about Susanna. Christopher's father, on the other hand, seems to have been an easygoing, popular man who occasionally got himself into trouble: He was elected to different committees in his guild and had many friends but also was briefly imprisoned for not paying his debts. He was even sued by his daughter Bianchinetta's fiancé for not paying the dowry he had promised. A dowry is an amount of money or, sometimes, valuable items—like jewelry or furniture—that a woman brings with her when she is married. The amount of the dowry was very important—often, a man would not agree to marry a woman unless her family gave her a large enough dowry. Sometimes, families would argue over dowries for months or years. In this case, the fiancé received the dowry, and he and Bianchinetta married.

The Colombos were members of a very small and lucky group during medieval times: the middle class. This group was fairly unusual at that time. The vast majority of people were very poor (the peasants). A few were very rich (the nobility). The Colombos were neither. They were solid, prosperous merchants with plenty to eat, a modest but sturdy home, and well-made clothes to wear.

School and Work

For such an extraordinary person, young Christopher had a very ordinary childhood. He attended the school for children of weavers run by Domenico's guild. Most sons of the merchants attended the school of their fathers' guild. Girls generally did not go to school, receiving what little education they could at home. Christopher learned reading, writing, basic arithmetic, and Latin at his grammar school. Medieval schools were not fun places—

As a child, Christopher attended a school similar to the one depicted in this medieval woodcut, c. 1498–1500, which depicts a schoolmaster and his students. The master holds a long wooden stick to help him keep order.

the school day lasted as long as thirteen hours and the teachers, who were called masters, regularly beat the students with sticks for fidgeting, misbehaving, or not knowing their lessons.

Though they attended school, learned lessons, and played games like children in modern times, children in the Middle Ages were viewed very differently than children today. Generally, they were seen as little adults from the time they could walk and talk. If they didn't go to school, children did the same work as adults all day. Christopher almost certainly worked for his father from a very young age, along with his siblings and his mother.

For such an extraordinary person, young Christopher had a very ordinary childhood.

Domenico was the only one who did the actual weaving of the wool. The rest of the family was in charge of carding the wool for spinning into yarn. Carding is the process through which the raw wool fibers are combed out straight and fine and all the dirt and grass bits are removed. The fibers are then spun by hand into thread with a spindle. So for many hours every day, Christopher would sit in his father's shop, scraping heavy wooden paddles with bristles together to make little fluffy balls of wool.

Hungry Desires

Perhaps it was these hours of labor that convinced Christopher that being a wool-weaver was not the life he wanted. We don't know exactly how and when this boy fell in love with the sea but we do know that for his entire life, Christopher desired two things above all: fame and wealth. The life of a weaver could offer him neither of these.

When he was a teenager, possibly around fourteen, Christopher left school and his father's workshop. He apprenticed himself to a merchant on a trading ship. No one knows what Domenico and Susanna felt about their son leaving the weaving trade, but most parents during those days expected their children to follow them in the family business. They may have been disappointed that Christopher had no interest in weaving.

In 1470, when he was only nineteen, Columbus sailed on his first long voyage on one of his employer's ships to the island of Chios in the Aegean Sea. Before this, he had most likely just made short runs to other ports nearby, never far from land. It was probably on this trip and a second Chios voyage in 1475 that Columbus first learned how to **navigate** and steer a ship through the open water on a long voyage—invaluable skills that he would spend the rest of his life refining.

The same year of Christopher's first long sailing trip, the whole family moved to Savona, a coastal town on the Italian Riviera. Domenico started a business selling local wines in addition to his weaving. By this time, Columbus was almost certainly taking small journeys along the coast on merchant ships, learning sailing skills, and navigating.

Though he still lived occasionally with his parents and helped his father with the wool business, during the early 1470s Columbus was working regularly for Genoese merchants, sailing their ships across the Mediterranean to Spain and France, and down to the North African coast.

Ambition and Determination

Columbus had been immersed in money-dealing and commercial transactions almost daily since his birth. He had spent his childhood and adolescence in his father's shop, watching the money-for-goods change hands. As a merchant's employee, he saw

Spices such as the nutmeg, cinnamon, cardamom, and anise shown in this photograph were brought to Europe by trading ships. In some cases, they were more valuable than gold.

the ships laden with precious trade goods, furs, gold, and spices. He saw the riches that successful trading could bring—and he knew that he wanted these riches also.

Even as a teenager, Columbus's most defining character trait was his incredible drive and determination. It isn't clear just from where this intense ambition sprang. Columbus probably didn't inherit these traits from his father. Though he had his weaving business and his sidelines in wine-selling and gate-keeping, Domenico wasn't an adventurer like his son. Like most people, he was content to live out his days in familiar surroundings—working, eating, talking with his neighbors and customers. Perhaps it was that very contentedness of his father that lit such a fire in Columbus to achieve the fantastic goals he set for himself.

Even as a teenager, Columbus's most defining character trait was his incredible drive and determination.

Columbus also spoke frequently about his desire to spread Christianity to **heathen** cultures. This was a popular cause during those times, but it was not necessarily based entirely on religious belief. Converting people in other countries also meant that European governments would be able to control them. The governments could have access to the valuable goods of those countries and even be able to rule them someday.

Some of this thinking may have sprung from the fall of Constantinople (the city known today as Istanbul) to the Ottoman Turks, only two years after Columbus was born. The land trade routes to the spices of the East were cut off and a huge area of formerly Christian-controlled territory was now in the hands of an Islamic empire. The cries to take back Jerusalem and the Holy Lands were heard everywhere in Europe. It would have been hard for young Columbus to avoid their influence.

Whatever their origins, the desires for money and fame would never leave Christopher Columbus, not even on the day of his death. These two overwhelming ambitions would spur him to actions that would eventually change the course of human civilization.

CHAPTER 2

The Seeds of an Idea

[Christopher] Columbus . . . decided to see the great ocean and left for Portugal.
—*Gonzalo Fernández de Oviedo*

By the time he was in his early twenties, Columbus had grown into a striking young man. He was tall, well above the five feet, seven inches that was average for men in the Middle Ages. He had broad, strong shoulders and muscular arms. His pale skin easily burned red in the sun. He had a hooked nose, pale blue eyes that looked even paler against his red face, and red-blond hair that had turned completely white by his early thirties.

Columbus had developed an intense, compelling personality. He was tough, adventurous, and not afraid of hard work, but he had a strong temper that he rarely tried to control. Most of all, the young man Columbus projected an air of absolute assurance: His friends remembered him as a man who knew exactly what he wanted.

In 1476, Columbus had an experience that would set him on the course of his life's plan. He was

This 19th-century engraving of the adult Christopher Columbus was originally on a piece of currency. He was always self-assured and knew what he wanted.

twenty-five and a crew member with a Genoese commercial trading fleet. They were carrying a valuable load of mastic, a resin used in varnishes. The ships were sailing near the southern coast of Portugal when they were suddenly attacked by thirteen French-Portuguese warships. Portugal and France were not at war with Genoa, so no one knows why the ships attacked. They may have wanted to steal the goods the Genoans were carrying. All day, the two fleets traded cannon and gunfire in fierce fighting. Just before nightfall, the ship Columbus was on burst into flames and sank. Most of the crew drowned. Columbus jumped off the deck of the sinking vessel, grabbed an oar floating nearby, and clung to it as he swam to shore.

He was beached near the tiny coastal fishing village of Lagos, Portugal. Kindly villagers dried his clothes and offered him food and a place to rest. Columbus eventually made his way to the bustling capital of Portugal, Lisbon, where he would spend the next ten years.

Life in Lisbon

Lisbon was the perfect place for a young, ambitious person to live. The commerce of the entire city centered on the shipping trade. Every week, beautifully crafted, powerful vessels would sail out of the harbor, loaded with trade goods. There was also a great push for sea exploration during these years, especially along the coast of Africa. New technologies were making ships sleeker, faster, and capable of carrying more provisions. They could stay out at sea longer than ever before.

With every journey, captains were pushing farther and farther along the African coast, gathering ivory and slaves along the way. When they returned, maps would be redrawn, incorporating the new coastlines, islands, and inlets the sailors reported. Spanish and Portuguese ships made regular trips to the Azores and Canary Islands, which lay near the coasts of Spain and Morocco.

Once settled in Lisbon, Columbus started sailing again on various commercial ships. He sailed north and south near the coast, learning how to handle the Atlantic currents and winds. He made a trip to the Madeira Islands near the Moroccan coast. He had the responsibility of negotiating the price for a load of sugar, purchasing the sugar, and returning with it safely. This was an important test for a young person just learning the ways of the business world.

Unfortunately, the trip did not go smoothly. For reasons that are unclear, Columbus's employer, a man named Paolo di Negro, only gave a portion of the money needed to buy the sugar to Columbus. When Columbus arrived in Madeira, the sugar sellers refused to give him the entire load even after Columbus promised them the rest of the money was forthcoming. Columbus had to return with only a small amount of the sugar. His employer was furious.

Christopher Columbus probably saw a scene much like this one when he made his way to Lisbon after the shipwreck. This 16th-century illustration was drawn by mapmakers Georg Braun and Franz Hogenberg.

During this period, Columbus also learned how to sail the two main types of long-distance sailing ships of the time: the caravel and the nao. Caravels were a new kind of ship that combined aspects of the big, sturdy, yet slower northern European trading ships with the sleeker, faster, narrower Mediterranean fishing ships. The nao was similar to the caravel but was heavier and slower. Later, Columbus would bring both of these types of ships with him on his historic journey.

Theories About the World

During his years in Lisbon, Columbus also operated a little mapmaking and bookselling shop with his brother Bartolomeo, who had followed him to the city. During his hours in his little shop, Columbus had the chance to study history and geography

An undated colored woodcut shows Columbus examining maps by lamplight during his time in Portugal. It was then that the explorer first began to study geography and astronomy.

for the first time in his life. He became especially interested in the ideas of Ptolemy, a Greek astronomer whose book *Geography* formed the basis for most of Europe's beliefs about the structure and size of the world.

During his hours in his little shop, Columbus had the chance to study history and geography for the first time in his life.

During the fifteenth century, everyone believed that the world was formed mainly of one giant landmass—Europe and Asia and Africa—surrounded by one enormous body of water they called the Ocean Sea. Every educated person also understood that the world was round. In addition, Ptolemy and other widely studied astronomers had calculated that the globe was far smaller than it really is.

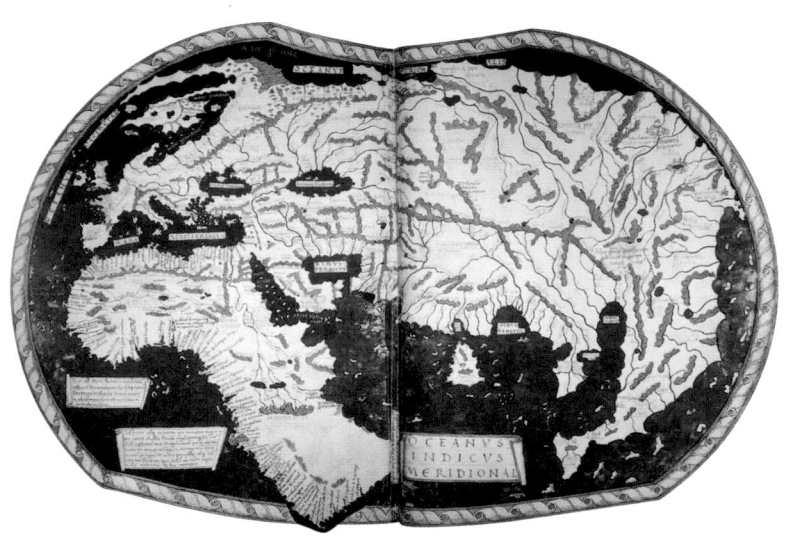

This world map, drawn by Henricus Martellus in 1489, shows how people of Columbus's day thought land on Earth was arranged. Columbus may have had access to this map when he formulated his grand plan.

A New Way to the Far East

During the 1200s, the explorer Marco Polo was one of the first Europeans to travel overland eastward from Europe through what is now the Middle East. He reached China and met the ruler, known as the Grand Khan. Over the next two centuries, trade amoung India and China and Europe increased. There was great demand for Eastern trade goods. However, the overland route, known as the Silk Road, was long and cumbersome. Travelers had to traverse deserts and mountains. Bandits and robbers lurked along the way. During the fifteenth century, the trade routes became blocked by the Ottoman Empire when it took over Constantinople.

The powerful ruler Kublai Khan, also called the Grand Khan, is depicted in this antique Chinese engraving.

Europe dreamed of finding another way to the East—the Indies, as they called it. Of course, one could sail south and then east around the tip of Africa, but sailing technology was not advanced enough to carry ships that far—and besides, no one really knew how large that continent actually was. There had to be another way.

Night after night, a candle burned in the window of Bartolomeo and Columbus's little bookshop. Columbus sat inside, bent over papers and books. He read and wrote and read some more until his eyes were red with exhaustion. The tiniest inkling of an idea was starting to grow, like a spark, deep in his mind. Soon, that little spark of an idea grew larger and consumed Columbus.

Marco Polo

During Marco Polo's time, China was ruled by the grandson of Genghis Khan, Kublai Khan, also known as the Grand Khan. The Khan liked the European explorer, and Marco Polo wound up staying at his court for seventeen years. He even served as the Khan's ambassador on various diplomatic missions in the region. When he returned, he wrote a book in which he described the fantastic riches of the Eastern lands—silks, jewels, valuable resins and gums, spices, and of course, gold. The book was very popular among educated Europeans and was widely circulated.

Explorer Marco Polo, shown in this engraving, stayed at the court of the Khan for seventeen years and wrote a book about his experiences.

CHAPTER 3

Hatching a Plan

[I]t happened that a lady whose name was Dona Felipa Moniz . . . was so taken with him, that she became his wife.

—*Fernando Columbus*

In 1477, Columbus took charge of a ship that was making a voyage to Iceland. Iceland was well known to the Europeans and was a regular stop on the commercial trade routes. It is possible that Columbus had visited the country before. On one of these trips, the young seaman may have heard the story of the Viking Leif Eriksson, an eleventh-century explorer who sailed west of Iceland into the unknown waters beyond.

The Vikings were not the only people to report reaching land by sailing westward across the sea, but Columbus may not have known of these other stories. In ancient times, people from coastal Africa occasionally returned from sea voyages with stories of being "blown" across—probably carried by the westerly trade winds—to the coast of what was most likely Brazil. Some Chinese legends told of a man named Hoei-Sin who sailed east and found a continent, which he called Fusang, where there were cacti growing. He might have been describing Mexico. Columbus had almost certainly heard the Azores fisherman tell of sighting *something* in the distance when they were fishing far off the western coast of the islands.

The Vikings

The Vikings, a group of warriors from Scandinavia, were skilled mariners and great explorers. Leif Eriksson's father was Erik the Red, a Viking leader famous for his red hair. Leif is thought to have been a big, tall man who inherited his father's flaming red hair.

During the eleventh century, Leif and his men had sailed west from Iceland and found a rocky, wooded land. They called this place Vinland for the currants, a berry-like fruit, they found there. Leif created a large, thriving settlement in this new place, which was probably modern-day Labrador, on the coast of Canada. However, native people attacked the settlement repeatedly. These people are the ancestors of the modern-day Inuit. In their writings, the Vikings refer to them as *skraelings*, which translates as "barbarians," or "pitiful wretches," according to some.

Far outnumbered, the Vikings returned to Iceland. The simple huts they had built crumbled in the wind. In only a few years, no sign was left that the Vikings had ever lived on that land.

The Vikings traveled on ships like the one shown here in their explorations westward from Iceland to Labrador.

Dreaming of the Big Idea

Columbus had a copy of Marco Polo's famous book, which he read many times and made notes in the margins. He was fascinated by Polo's descriptions of the incredible riches of the Grand Khan's empire: rubies as big as a man's fist, palaces with floors of gold two inches thick, forests of trees dripping with gums and resins. He did not seem to care that the accounts of the Grand Khan he was reading were now more than two hundred years old and might be outdated— or even exaggerated. That tiny spark was beginning to grow brighter in his mind, fed with ambition. Was it—*could* it be possible to sail *west across the world* to reach the Indies?

He was fascinated by Polo's descriptions of the incredible riches of the Grand Khan's empire.

This was an intoxicating idea. If he could figure out how to do it, to sail west across the Ocean Sea and reach the eastern shores of the Indies, *if* he could do that incredible feat that no one else had ever done, well! He would be rich and famous beyond belief! He would be able to bring back shiploads of gold and spices. The news of his achievement would bring him acclaim wherever he went, for the rest of his life and the rest of his family's life. The name *Columbus* would be forever linked with unthinkable wealth and power.

Hoei-Sin described cacti similar to the type shown here, photographed in Arizona's Saguaro National Park.

Making the Numbers "Work"

Could he do it? Columbus asked himself. His favorite astronomer and geographer, Ptolemy, had written that he had figured out how big Earth was and how much of it was land and how much water. He wrote that the landmass we know today as Eurasia stretched over fifty percent of Earth's circumference, with ocean making up the rest. Actually, there is far less land and more ocean than this. Even with Ptolemy's calculations though, no one could carry enough food and water to sail across the sea and Columbus knew it. Therefore, he decided that, in his opinion, Ptolemy's calculations were wrong.

In Columbus's mind, a French astrologer named Pierre d'Ailly was the person who had the right numbers. D'Ailly said that the Eurasian landmass was actually much bigger, stretching over sixty percent of Earth's surface, which made the area of

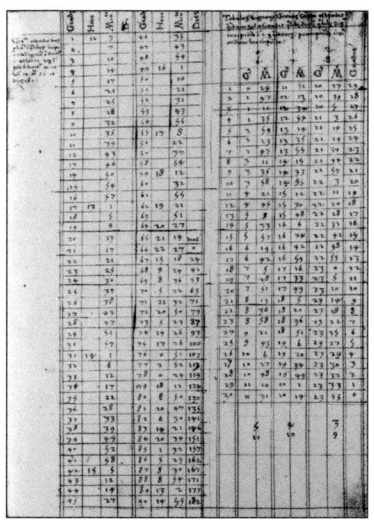

This is an image of Columbus's own copy of Pierre d'Ailly's *Imago Mundi*. Columbus studied this book intensely, making notes in the margin, which are visible here. This particular page has a table depicting the length of the days at different latitudes.

water smaller. In reality, d'Ailly was even farther off in his land and water assumptions than Ptolemy, but Columbus didn't know that and chose to use d'Ailly's calculations.

Even using d'Ailly's calculations, Columbus could see that there was still too much ocean to cross. However, he wanted so much for his plan to work that he was willing to twist some of the numbers to suit himself. He decided that all of the calculations he had been studying must have been in "Roman miles," which were much shorter than the nautical miles he had previously assumed they were calculated in.

Columbus convinced himself that the distance he had to sail to reach China and India was about 2,700 nautical miles. This was a magical number: It meant that ships could carry enough food and water to sustain a crew from coast to coast on the journey. This was the key Columbus had been seeking.

A Noble Marriage

During the year 1479, Columbus went to a Mass at the chapel of the Convento dos Santos, "the Convent of the Saints," in Lisbon. This was not just any chapel though. The convent was also a boarding school for highborn daughters of the Portuguese aristocracy. The young ladies attended Mass at the chapel, which had gained a reputation as a popular place for young men to choose a wife. During Mass, Columbus noticed a young woman named Felipa Perestrello e Moniz.

Felipa was the eldest daughter of a noble Portuguese family, and she was already twenty-five years old when she met Columbus—almost too old to be married. In those days, young girls frequently married during their teens. Felipa's father was dead and Felipa's mother had found herself cheated of much of her fortune by her own son, Bartolomeo Perestrello II.

This may have been one reason Felipa reached the age of twenty-five before finding a husband—she could bring little or no dowry to a marriage.

Apparently, this lack of dowry didn't matter to Columbus. Felipa had something he wanted even more than money—she had aristocratic connections, which Columbus both desired for himself and needed for his

Royalty were the only ones with that much money, and they would be much more likely to listen to his ideas if they knew he had married into a noble family.

mission. Her mother's family, the Monizes, was one of the oldest noble families in the region. Felipa's father, Bartolomeo Perestrello I, was an Italian aristocrat who had been appointed governor of one of the Madeira Islands by Prince Henry of Portugal. Prince Henry was the son of King João of Portugal—a link that could potentially be very useful, Columbus may have thought. If he were going to

This rare antique engraving depicts Prince Henry of Portugal, also called Prince Henry the Navigator, who was acquainted with Felipa's father.

A 1485 woodcut shows a couple dancing at their wedding, as Columbus and Felipa might have done when they were married.

push forward with his scheme, he would also need financial backers. Royalty were the only ones with that much money, and they would be much more likely to listen to his ideas if they knew he had married into a noble family.

However, it seems that Felipa loved Columbus. One of Columbus's sons, Fernando, grew up to be his father's biographer. He wrote of his father's courtship with Felipa, "For as much as he behaved himself honorably, and was a man of comely presence, and did nothing but what was just; it happened that a lady whose name was Dona Felipa Moniz . . . was so taken with him, that she became

Columbus had two sons, shown in this medieval portrait. Diego was born in 1480 to Felipa Perestrello e Moniz, and Fernando was born in 1488 to Beatriz Enriquez de Arana.

his wife." However, no one knows if Columbus loved his wife in return—he never wrote of their courtship or marriage. He never mentioned Felipa's name in any of his journals and diaries—they are filled instead with dreams of exploration.

In 1479, Felipa and Columbus wed. Within a year of their marriage, their first and only child was born, a boy named Diego. Soon after they were married, the Columbuses moved to the Madeira Islands to live with Felipa's family. Her brother, Bartolomeo, was now the governor of Porto Santo, the same island his father had governed. Felipa's mother lived with Bartolomeo on the island, even though he had cheated her years earlier. She probably had nowhere else to live.

Gathering More Evidence

While he was living on the island, Columbus heard many tales about certain pieces of driftwood that had washed ashore and were "ingeniously carved, but not by iron." Odd hollow pieces of cane had washed up, so thick they could hold quarts of wine, the people said. They found tree trunks of a different type than they had ever seen before. Most tantalizing of all, the people told Columbus of "two dead bodies with broad faces and different in appearance from the Christians," as Fernando wrote many years later.

Some scholars have also speculated that while he was living in Madeira, Columbus may have received secret information from a close friend about lands far west across the ocean. This sailor, who is sometimes called the Unknown Pilot, is said to have entrusted Columbus with this secret just before he died. To present day, historians have been unable to find any evidence of this incident, except for what is written by some of Columbus's early biographers.

Some scholars have also speculated that . . . Columbus may have received secret information from a close friend about lands far west across the ocean.

Columbus gained another unexpected boost to his idea. Bartolomeo Perestrello I, Felipa's father, had been a seafaring man. When Columbus's mother-in-law learned of her new son-in-law's interest in ocean exploration, she produced her late husband's sea journals and charts. No one knows just what was in these documents, but Columbus's early biographers wrote that they made him very excited. It seems that the papers hinted at lands across the Ocean Sea. The spark burst into flame.

The Legend of the Unknown Pilot

Gonzalo Fernández de Oviedo was one of Columbus's biographers. In his 1535 book, *General and Natural History of the Indies*, he tells the story of the Unknown Pilot. A Portuguese caravel was sailing from Spain to England, he says, and was driven off course by a storm. The ship was forced to sail with the westward winds for many days until the sailors spotted land. They anchored and went ashore, where they found people who did not wear any clothes. The sailors soon left and began sailing home, but during the journey back to Portugal, almost all of the crew died—except for the pilot, and he was very ill. He found his way to Madeira, for reasons no one knows. Before he died, he told his close friend Christopher Columbus of the lands he had seen and asked Columbus to draw a map. Then he died, leaving his friend with this magical story.

This statue of Columbus biographer Oviedo stands in Santo Domingo in the Dominican Republic. Oviedo accompanied Columbus on his later voyages and then wrote about the adventures.

CHAPTER 4

Columbus at the Court

*First, Your Highnesses . . . appoint Sir Christopher
from now on as your admiral on all those islands
and mainland discovered . . .*

> —*The Capitulations of April 17*

Once he had his scheme in place, Christopher Columbus
never doubted for one instant that he *could* and *would* sail
west across the Ocean Sea to
find the empire of the Grand
Khan in the Indies. This sort
of unblinking self-confidence
was typical of Columbus. He
rarely, if ever, doubted himself

> *He rarely, if ever,
> doubted himself and he
> rarely admitted
> mistakes.*

and he rarely admitted mistakes. Once he decided that he
wanted something, he did not waver for one moment in his
quest to get it. This blind ambition would serve him well
over the next months and years.

Columbus knew that the next step in realizing his
dream was to find and secure some financial backers. His
own family, of course, had no accumulated wealth and
Felipa's family was noble but poor. Just like any modern-
day **entrepreneur** with a brilliant idea, Columbus needed
someone to invest money in his idea in return for a share
of the profits. He would need ships, provisions, a crew,
and money to pay for them. However, there was something
he wanted more than money.

Columbus also wanted **sovereignty** over the lands he might find across the ocean. He wanted the title that would go with such a position *and* a share of whatever wealth would be on the islands *and* the ability to create colonies in the new land that he would govern. The only people who could offer him such terms were royalty. Some people might have been afraid to approach kings and queens with such grand requests. Timidity was not one of Columbus's problems.

Seeking Support from the King of Portugal

Sometime after Diego's birth and before 1484, Felipa died. No one knows what she died of or even exactly when. She was buried at the Carmo convent near Lisbon. Columbus did not write about his wife's death, and his early biographers noted it only in passing. Whether he mourned her or not, Columbus would not be deterred from his goal.

In 1484, Columbus journeyed to the court of King João of Portugal. He took his son Diego with him, even though the boy was only four or five years old. Since Felipa's death, the only person left to Diego was his father. João received the Genoan Columbus and listened to his plan. He was intrigued, being interested in ocean exploration himself. After conferring with his advisors, though, he concluded that Columbus was not basing his plans on reality but instead on imagination, as the court historian noted. Moreover, he was put off by this man's boasting and arrogance. He sent Columbus on his way.

For reasons no one really knows, Columbus left Portugal secretly. He was apparently afraid that the king's men would come after him. Some historians speculate that he may have gone into debt for various living expenses during his time at the court and was trying to leave without paying.

In this painting, the artist imagines Columbus dreaming of sailing while his young son Diego sits by his side. Diego accompanied his father to Portugal when Columbus met with King João.

From Portugal, it must have seemed natural to go next door to that other great seafaring nation, Spain. Here, Columbus felt the monarchs would surely be more receptive.

Meeting Ferdinand and Isabella of Spain

The Spanish monarchs, Queen Isabella and King Ferdinand, were an impressive couple. Isabella of Castile was a beautiful woman with long auburn hair. She was a devout Catholic with a strong interest in converting "heathen" cultures. She was known for being both aggressive and smart, and her marriage to Ferdinand of Aragon united the two kingdoms and created what is known today as modern Spain. Ferdinand was a short man with a big barrel chest. He loved sports and athletics and was known for being ruthless in war and brilliant and scheming when making deals.

Queen Isabella, shown in this c. 1496–1519 painting, was married to King Ferdinand of Aragon.

Together, the monarchs ruled over a wealthy and powerful Spain tightly controlled by the Catholic Church. They had no official site for their court but instead traveled with an enormous **entourage** from place to place throughout their country, tending to the problems of each region. In 1485, when Columbus first sought them out, the court was residing at the castle of Alcazar in the south. The massive yellow stone palace was a magnificent place, surrounded by miles of lush gardens. No doubt Columbus felt this was a fitting spot for his equally magnificent plea.

He had to wait several months, however, for the monarchs to return from a trip. When they finally agreed to receive him, the meeting did not go well. Columbus's timing was off. The monarchs were deep in the midst of a war to wrestle the last section of Spain away from the Moorish Arabs who had held it for centuries. They were consumed by military details. Isabella's mind was fixed on the hundreds of new subjects who would be converted to Catholicism once Spain had won. They had little time to spare for this proud man standing before them with his bold scheme of sailing to the Indies. In addition, he was requesting such terms! Sovereignty over all the lands he found, title of Admiral of the Ocean Sea, and ten percent of all the profits were just a few!

Still, his plan was intriguing. Access to the Indies by sea would mean great riches, of course, but also an edge over all of the other countries in Europe if Spain could do it first. This man Columbus was intriguing, too. He projected a powerful aura of magnetism and absolute confidence. Ferdinand and Isabella decided not to dismiss Columbus immediately. They ordered a commission of experts to study Columbus's plan. It did not take the group long to agree that Columbus's calculations were all wrong. In their opinion, the Ocean Sea was far vaster than he was proposing. There would be no way for a man to sail west to eastern lands without dying from lack of food and water.

A 19th-century photograph shows the interior of the Hall of Ambassadors at Alcazar in Spain.

This painting, c. 1888, depicts Columbus, surrounded by members of the court, pleading his case to King Ferdinand and Queen Isabella. He wanted them to finance an exploration to the Indies.

Somehow though, probably by sheer force of will, Columbus—watching his life's plan tremble in the balance—managed to convince the committee not to reject him outright but to reconsider some time in the future. To ensure that Columbus would not leave and take his scheme—however improbable—to another monarch, Columbus was given a small amount of money to live on and allowed to remain at the court.

Years of Pleading

Thus began what must have been the most difficult period of Columbus's life so far. He wound up waiting for eight years at the Spanish court, hanging on by a thread. Occasionally, he would be granted an audience with the monarchs at which he would plead his case anew but was otherwise ignored. He was tortured by the idea that someone might steal his plan and sail to the Indies before him. Still, he could not move on; there was always the chance that his petition would be granted.

Columbus's brother Bartolomeo tried to help by seeking out another monarch to sponsor Columbus. While Columbus continued to wait in the Spanish court, Bartolomeo traveled to England and had an audience with King Henry VII but was rejected. Then he tried France, where the older sister of King Charles VIII took an interest in him but not enough to convince the king to support Columbus's scheme.

Like the king and queen of Spain, King Henry VII of England also rejected Columbus's case.

Columbus didn't spend all of his time at court just waiting around, though. He would frequently visit a certain **apothecary**'s shop where scientists, physicians, and surgeons regularly met for conversation. Columbus enjoyed their talks and dropped by sometimes to join their conversations. While he was there, a friend of Columbus's introduced him to a young peasant woman who was a **ward** of his family. Beatriz Enriquez de Arana was twenty years old, and she and Columbus were instantly attracted to each another. The two began a relationship, and in 1488 she bore his son Fernando, who would grow up to accompany his famous father on his voyages and become his biographer.

Columbus met Beatriz in the shop of an apothecary, like this one depicted in a 14th-century medical textbook.

In 1490, the royal committee commissioned to study Columbus's scheme officially rejected him—once and for all, they said. His plan would never work and would be a waste of money. Still, Columbus refused to give up. Isabella had become quite fond of him during his years at the court, so he appealed to her alone. Despite the commission's conclusion, she told him that perhaps she would think about it after the war with the Moors was over, but right now, she was much too busy.

Beatriz Enriquez de Arana

Beatriz was in some ways the love of Columbus's life. According to records, theirs was the only relationship Columbus had after the death of his wife, Felipa. The two never married, most likely because she was not of noble blood. For someone as status-conscious as Columbus, a wife who could not appear at the royal court would be unthinkable. Columbus never forgot her, though. In a will he dictated the day before his death, he specifically provided for her care, saying "She weighs heavily on my conscience. The reason for this I am not permitted to write here."

CHRISTOFEL COLONUS.

This medieval engraving shows Christopher Columbus as a middle-aged man. Although he never married Beatriz, he thought of her even when he was near death.

In 1492, Columbus was forty-one years old. He had seen more of the world than most people but his life's dream seemed perpetually on hold. However, his fortunes were soon to shift. That year, after more than two centuries, the last stronghold of Islam in Spain fell when the Catholic army marched into the Alhambra fortress at Granada. The Moorish War was over. At last! Columbus must have thought. Now the king and queen could turn their minds to his quest. He was right. Several days later, Columbus stood before the monarchs and received the final blow. They had considered his scheme again, Ferdinand and Isabella told him, and they were rejecting it—permanently.

This 1868 wood engraving by British artist John Gilbert shows a balding and bearded Columbus pointing to a map with Isabella and Ferdinand watching.

It was too risky for the amount of money they would have to lay out but mostly, they simply could not accept the incredible conditions he was demanding if they did fund the voyage. This was their final word.

Columbus was devastated. He had given eight years of his life to waiting, eight years of hoping. There was no time to waste. Columbus packed up and left the court. He was going to France. Perhaps Charles VIII would give him another chance.

A Change of Royal Heart

Back at the court, however, events were turning. During his time at court, Columbus had made friends with Luis de Santangel, the queen's treasurer. De Santangel believed in Columbus but more than that, he was a "numbers" man. He knew that the voyage could bring huge potential rewards for comparatively little money—even with Columbus's demands.

As Columbus rode away on his mule, de Santangel argued with the queen, telling her that she had made a mistake in dismissing Columbus. De Santangel was Isabella's trusted advisor, and he seemed very sure of himself. Perhaps she and Ferdinand had been wrong in rejecting Columbus, Isabella thought. Perhaps they were passing up a great opportunity, especially when considering all those potential souls in faraway lands that could be converted to Catholicism.

He had given eight years of his life to waiting, eight years of hoping.

A royal messenger was summoned. Isabella ordered him to find the man Columbus and bring him back to the court—quickly, before he got any farther away. With a pounding of hooves, dust flying, the messenger raced through villages and across fields. He didn't have far to go. In the little hamlet of Pinos Puente, only a few miles from the court, he found Columbus mounted on his humble mule, making his way to France, weary and heartsick.

Surely, in all of Columbus's wildest imaginings, he never thought this possible. He turned around right there in the middle of the road and rode back to the palace with the messenger. It had happened at last! His dream was coming true. Now he just had to get the monarchs to agree to his conditions—that was almost as important as the journey itself.

Negotiating with the King and Queen

Isabella, Ferdinand, and Columbus negotiated the terms of the contract for three months. As in any modern business deal, they argued over the amounts of the profits, who would hold the rights over the lands found, what sort of ships would be used, and how they would be outfitted.

On April 17, 1492, the negotiations finally drew to a close. Everyone signed a contract, which is known in history as the Capitulations of April 17. It stated that in return for finding the empire of the Khan, Columbus would have rights to one-tenth of all the gold, silver, pearls, gems, gums, and spices he might find. He would be the governor of any islands and mainland he might find. He would also be awarded the grand-sounding title "Admiral of the Ocean Sea." The contract stated that the title would be passed down to Columbus's descendants. This was important to Columbus and was one of the key points to which he had hoped the monarchs would agree. He would at last shed the mantle of Christopher, son of Domenico the wool-weaver, to become a noble. More importantly, passing on the title ensured that his place in history would be preserved.

Excerpts from the Capitulations

The Capitulations were worded as a request from Columbus to the monarchs. The following is an excerpt from the Capitulations:

"For what he will discover on the voyage that now, with the help of God, he is to make on the Ocean Seas in the service of Your Highnesses are the following: First, Your Highnesses, as the lords you are of the Ocean Seas, appoint Sir Christopher from now on as your admiral on all those islands and mainland discovered or acquired by his [Columbus's] command and expertise in the Ocean Seas during his lifetime and, after his death, by his heirs and successors one after the other in perpetuity . . . Also, Your Highnesses appoint Sir Christopher your viceroy and governor general in all those islands and any mainland and islands that he may discover and acquire in the seas . . . You wish him to have and take for himself one-tenth of all and any merchandise, whether pearls, precious stones, gold, silver, spices, and any other things and merchandise of whatever kind, name, or sort it may be, that is bought, exchanged, found, acquired, and obtained . . . These are authorized and dispatched with the replies from Your Highnesses at the end of each article. In the town of Santa Fe de La Vega de Granada, on the seventeenth day of April in the year of the birth of our savior Jesus Christ one thousand four hundred and ninety-two."

This is the signature of Queen Isabella, as would have been found on the Capitulations of April 17.

CHAPTER 5

Planning the Journey

Your Highnesses ordained that I should not go eastward by land in the usual manner but by the western way which no one about whom we have positive information has ever followed.

Columbus wrote constantly of the upcoming voyage in his journal. In almost every single entry, he lovingly described the gold he knew he would find. This voyage across the sea was to be made entirely for profit. Columbus was not a scientist or a geographer interested in plants and animals of foreign lands. He was a businessman, and his entire trip was planned based on the incredible riches he had no doubt he would discover in the kingdom of the Grand Khan.

No one, including the monarchs or Columbus, believed that he would have any trouble taking possession of the Khan's land and riches— after all, Spaniards already had experience taking over kingdoms in Africa.

Columbus—and many other Europeans— believed the Grand Khan to be a very rich man, as this 1868 drawing shows. The Khan is depicted going into battle riding four elephants.

The rulers encountered in Africa were so overwhelmed that they usually gave away anything the Europeans wanted without protest. Surely, the Khan and his people would be just as easy to subdue.

Acquiring the Ships

May 1492 found Columbus in the port city of Palos on the Spanish coast. Here, he would hire his crew and outfit his ships. Palos was a small port town that owed a debt to the crown for some undefined wrongdoing. The town was to repay its debt, the monarchs decreed, by supplying Columbus with two fully outfitted ships and all the necessary supplies for his journey. The town was not very happy about all of this bother and expense but could not argue.

As preparations moved forward, Columbus decided he needed a third ship. The monarchs had instructed Palos to

This undated painting shows the nao *Santa Maria*—Columbus's lead ship and his least favorite—riding the ocean waves.

provide Columbus with only two ships, but he needed more room for quarters for himself and extra food and water. Probably drawing on his personal funds, he arranged to rent a nao that happened to be moored in the Palos harbor.

The nao was christened the *Santa Maria*. The other two ships were the *Niña* and the *Pinta*. They were both lighter, sleeker caravels. The *Santa Maria* would turn out to have been a poor choice. Throughout the journey, Columbus frequently complained about its clumsiness and slowness. The swift little *Niña* would become his favorite ship.

> *The nao was christened the* Santa Maria. *The other two ships were the* Niña *and the* Pinta.

Assembling the Crew

Columbus had a hard time finding crewmembers at first: Not many men were eager to risk their lives on a journey that almost everyone considered completely insane. Who ever heard of sailing west to the Indies? In addition, most medieval Europeans believed that many lands of the world were populated by monstrous races of people: people completely covered with hair, people whose skin was blue, those who had faces in the middle of their chests and no heads, those who were giants or one-eyed cyclopes, or who ate human flesh. Aside from the usual dangers of an ocean voyage—storms, getting lost, lack of fresh water or food—why would anyone want to voluntarily sail off to the land of monsters? By alternately pleading, ordering, and threatening, Columbus eventually eked out ninety crewmembers for his three ships.

In addition to trustworthy ships and plenty of men, Columbus also needed excellent captains for the voyage. He found them in

Many sailors on Columbus's ships were afraid of meeting monsters like this mythical cyclops.

the two Pinzón brothers of Palos: Martin Alonso and Vicente Yañez. The brothers were important men in Palos. They were rich, well known, and influential. Martin Alonso in particular was one of the most respected sea captains in town.

Martin believed in Columbus's quest at a time when almost no one else did. He was in his mid-to upper-forties at the time of the journey—perhaps he was hoping for a glorious adventure and discovery with which to end his captaining career. He volunteered to captain the *Pinta* and he convinced Vicente Yañez, his younger brother, to serve as captain of the *Niña*. Columbus

Vicente Pinzón, shown in this painting composed of tiles, was the younger of the two Pinzón brothers and the captain of the *Niña*.

VICENTE YAÑEZ PINZON
(1460-1514)
CAPITAN DE LA CARABELA NIÑA.
DESCUBRIDOR DEL BRASIL Y EL AMAZONAS.
CAPITAN GENERAL Y CORREGIDOR DE LA ISLA
DE PUERTO RICO.
EXCMO.AYUNTAMIENTO DE PALOS DE LA FRONTERA

himself would captain the *Santa Maria*. The brothers, however, contributed more to the quest than just their sailing knowledge. It was probably because of their involvement that the townspeople in Palos even obeyed Columbus's demands at all, no matter what the crown ordered.

The sailors were quite apprehensive about this journey. Most had just sailed north and south along the coasts of Europe and Africa, never out of sight of land. What monstrous beings might they encounter on the way to the Indies? How would the admiral find the land? Would they ever return?

Crew of the First Voyage

Twenty-four men were entered into the ship's logbook for the *Niña*, twenty-six for the *Pinta*, and forty for the *Santa Maria*. Most of these were the common sailors who would be responsible for carrying out the orders of the captains and officers, cleaning the ship, repairing ropes and rigging, and fishing along the way. Only men were allowed to be sailors. There were no women at all on board any of the ships.

A secretary came along, as well as an interpreter who spoke Arabic, so that they could communicate with the Khan and his people. There were also barrel makers, caulkers, and carpenters to fix the ships, and a surgeon to provide the men with medical help.

In this painting, Columbus's crew, who was responsible for all aspects of the ships, pushes off from the Palos dock in a rowboat. The caravels wait in the background.

CHAPTER 6

Life on the Ocean Sea

Half an hour before sunrise . . . I departed on a course for the Canary Islands. . . . I intended to set out and sail until I reached the Indies.

Finally, all of the arrangements were complete. The sailors were onboard. The officers were stationed on the decks. At a command from their captains, each ship spread its massive sails. Slowly, they pulled out of Palos harbor. It was August 3, 1492.

In this 1893 chromolithograph, the artist imagines Christopher Columbus saying good-bye to Isabella as he leaves on the first voyage. In reality, however, it is doubtful that Isabella was in Palos at the time of Columbus's departure.

The crew was first bound for the Canary Islands, near the coast of Spain. The *Pinta's* rudder needed repairs, and they could take on a few more provisions there. From the islands, Columbus thought he could pick up winds blowing west—and he was right. In the end, those winds carried the ships all the way across the Atlantic Ocean.

On September 6, 1492, the *Santa Maria*, the *Niña*, and the *Pinta*, with its new rudder, sailed off the coast of the Canary Islands heading west-southwest. The *Santa Maria*, though the slowest ship, almost certainly sailed in the front, with Columbus at the **bow**.

As the first days of the journey passed, the officers and crew settled into the routine of life at sea. They would end up sailing for about forty-three days. This may not sound like a very long time in an era when people can spend three months onboard a cruise ship. However, with the living conditions on medieval ships, forty-three days was a very long time!

Today, sailors have bathrooms on their vessels with showers and toilets. They have kitchens with sinks and stoves and refrigerators, and sleeping quarters with beds to sleep in, all made up with sheets and pillows and blankets. Of course, the biggest difference is that all modern ships sailing on business are powered by gasoline engines that can plow through the toughest storms and the calmest days.

Engines, running water, and refrigeration would not be invented for another four hundred and fifty years. Columbus was sailing three of the most technologically advanced ships available in the world, and they were all powered entirely by wind. If there was no wind, they didn't go anywhere. In fact, for several days at the start of his trip, the ships were **becalmed** near the Canary Islands, just a few miles from the coast. Everyone had to wait until the wind finally picked up.

Columbus's ships were entirely wind-powered, thanks to massive, carefully arranged sails like those depicted in this photograph. Without wind, the ships would be stalled at sea.

Life on Board the Ships

Being becalmed was the least of the crew's worries. Keeping the food edible and free from vermin was a major concern. Columbus had stocked his storage rooms with olive oil, vinegar, cheese, raisins, rice, chickpeas, lentils, and beans. These provisions had to last through the voyage and into the time on land, so they were carefully rationed.

Sailors spent a great deal of time trying to keep the rats and mice out of the bins, as well as the weevils and other insects that infested the storage rooms. There was a very limited amount of salted meat. They mostly caught fresh fish over the sides of the boats and salted and dried it. The job of the ship's cook would not be invented for another two hundred years, so if the sailors

Weevils, such as the one pictured here, and other vermin plagued Columbus's sailors throughout their voyages.

wanted to eat, they had to do their own cooking. The men would make biscuits from the weevil-filled flour and cook them over fires made in sandboxes on the deck so as not to set the ship on fire. Despite their best efforts, the food was rotten most of the time. The sailors would season everything with huge amounts of garlic to mask the taste. Sometimes, they would wait until after nightfall to eat so they wouldn't have to see the maggots in their food.

Poor food and nutrition were only a part of the sailors' difficult sea life. Space was very cramped. Only the captains had their own cabins and even those were tiny closets with room only for a cot and a small table. The common sailors slept on the decks, which must have been damp and cold at night.

The ships were filthy. Every person, including the admiral, had lice. Fleas and their hosts— the rats—were everywhere. There was no plumbing whatsoever, so everyone,

The ships were filthy. Every person, including the admiral, had lice.

including the captains and officers, relieved themselves over the side of the ship, perched on a crude wooden seat that extended over the ship's edge.

The sailors' clothes were just as dirty as their environment. Everyone wore the same set of clothing from the day they set sail until the day they returned to Europe—months at a time. This wasn't unusual though: In medieval days, all but the very wealthy only owned one or, at most, two sets of clothes at a time. All the crewmembers wore leggings, a woolen smock with a hood to protect against the salt spray, and a red cap called a *gorro*. This cap was the only thing that distinguished a sailor from any other man. Everyone went barefoot. No one was much bothered, though, by the food or the cramped spaces. This was all a normal part of life at sea.

Threat of Mutiny

In fact, the journey was going quite well—at least according to Columbus. The weather was excellent, he noted in his journal, and the ships were making good time. By generally holding the ship west-southwest, he was *certain* that they would run smack into the eastern coast of China or at least some of its outlying islands.

The crew, on the other hand, wasn't so sure. As they streamed ahead, each day put more miles of endless blue ocean between themselves and home. No one had ever sailed this long before, and yet there was still no sign of land. Everyone began getting nervous and restless. How would they ever get home after sailing so far? The admiral did not seem concerned, but what did he know?

Each day, their agitation grew. Their muttering increased. Late at night, some of the sailors began plotting a **mutiny**. They could sneak up on their admiral and pitch him overboard at night as he gathered coordinates by the North Star. Then they could turn the ships around and sail straight home.

Columbus spent much time and energy ensuring that his crew obeyed him. This lithograph shows the captain general surrounded by his men.

Calming the Sailors' Fears

It did not take Columbus long to hear of the sailors' unrest. He knew he had to keep them quiet and contented or risk ending the expedition and possibly his life. He devised a system in which he began keeping *two* logbooks: In one, he recorded the actual distance the ships had traveled each day. This book was for his eyes only. In the second logbook, he recorded fake numbers, reducing the daily distances by many miles. This book he shared nightly with the sailors to put a stop to their worry that they were going too far, too fast. This deception didn't bother Columbus at all. It was just like when he twisted the math to calculate the distance across the sea. Concealing the truth, or even outright lying, was not a problem for him—as long as he was getting his way. His captains and other experienced sailors probably knew these numbers weren't accurate but would not dare to contradict their admiral.

Soon though, the crew was distracted by the various sea plants and animals they encountered. The ships had sailed into what is known today as the Sargasso Sea. In this area of the Atlantic Ocean near what is today known as Bermuda, huge floating mats of seaweed create a habitat teeming with crabs, fish, birds, and other life. The sailors crowded the decks, shouting and pointing to the different animals they saw. They caught a small crab and a few birds with nets.

Eager for any indication that they were headed in the right direction, Columbus wrote in his journal that they must be close to land, because the seaweed seemed to be recently ripped from a

Columbus and his crew were excited when they sailed into the Sargasso Sea. Unfortunately, they were still hundreds of miles from land.

A False Log

In this excerpt from his logbook, Columbus writes of altering the distances to keep his men quiet. He refers to himself in the third person.

"Monday, 24 September: He sailed on his westward course fourteen and a half leagues [a league is about three miles] and reckoned twelve . . .

Tuesday, 25 September: They had sailed four and a half leagues westwards that day. That night, they went seventeen leagues south-west, a total of twenty-one. The Admiral, according to his custom, told the men they had gone thirteen leagues, for he was still afraid that they would consider the voyage too long. Thus throughout the voyage he kept two reckonings, one false and the other true."

shoreline. He was wrong, unfortunately. The ships were still more than seven hundred and fifty miles from land. The Sargasso's seaweed floats many miles above the ocean floor on the surface of the water. Columbus also noted that two birds he saw—a junco and a tern—were land birds and so therefore, landfall could not be far away. In fact, these birds are known to fly hundreds of miles from land.

Columbus was blissfully oblivious to his mistakes, though. Soon, he was sure they would be approaching the shores of the Indies, where wondrous riches awaited.

CHAPTER 7

Tierra, Tierra!

All of the men I saw were young . . . .
They were very well built with fine bodies
and handsome faces.

On October 21 by the **Gregorian calendar** used today, October 12 by Columbus's **Julian calendar**, the lookout stationed high on the mast of the *Pinta* spied what they had all been waiting for. "Tierra, tierra!" he cried out. "Land, land!" The men rushed the decks, crowding the rails, all shouting. They had traveled thirty-six days since leaving the Canary Islands. Most had been sure they would never again see the familiar sight of land emerging from the sea: the faint, bumpy brown line in the distance, slowly growing larger, trees emerging, the sand of the beach. At that moment, each man onboard thought that he had never seen anything so beautiful.

An artist imagines Columbus and his crew first sighting land in this colored woodcut.

Columbus's heart filled with triumph. His throat swelled so that it nearly choked him. There it was, just as he knew it would be—the Indies! Against all odds, he had sailed west—and had reached the East. His face scarlet with emotion, he turned and shouted to his men to drop the anchors and roll up the sails. They would sit offshore until the next day.

The night the crew spent anchored offshore must have been a suspenseful one for the men. They wondered what would await them onshore. Perhaps endless gold mines? Perhaps the palaces of the Grand Khan with floors of gold two inches thick and all the subjects arrayed in silk and brocade? Perhaps spices and piles of rubies, diamonds, and pearls as big as a man's fist? Perhaps **aloes** and mastic as precious as gold itself? Would they be greeted by the monsters they had heard so much about—the men with one eye or faces in the middle of their chests?

At the first sign of light, Columbus, his two captains, and their highest officers dressed in their finest regalia. They collected all the items they would need in order to take possession of the land before them: a standard— the official banner of the expedition—with green crosses and the royal emblems of Ferdinand and Isabella, and most importantly, plenty of weapons—swords, long staffs tipped with iron spikes, axes, and knives. They were prepared

This 1871 engraving by an American artist shows the historic moment when Columbus and his crew approached the island in a small boat.

to use force to claim the land, but they also stocked their rowboats with sailors' red caps and glass beads to offer as gifts if the people turned out to be peaceful. The men climbed down ropes on the sides of the ships into small rowboats, and they set off to change the world forever.

Inhabitants of the New Land

Of course, at that point, the ships were more than eight thousand miles from China, Japan, and India. They were near the coast of what is today known as Watling Island, in the Bahamas. All of the Caribbean islands—including the Bahamas, Haiti, the Dominican Republic, and Cuba—were settled in those days by a group of people who called themselves *Taínos*, and they were most certainly not subjects of the Grand Khan or any Khan at all. Their world was as different from the Indies as a humble pond was from the Ocean Sea itself.

The Taínos populated the islands of the Caribbean, shown here on a historic map. The region used to be known as the "Spanish Main."

The Taínos were the entire population of these islands and so far, they had lived completely isolated from the rest of the world. Their lives were peaceful and harmonious. They lived on islands filled with abundance and beauty. The land was lush and tropical, with beaches, lowland forests, mountains, and rivers and lakes scattered throughout. The summers were warm and rainy and the winters generally cool and dry. These islands had been good to the Taínos. They had plenty to eat, snug homes, and enough leisure time to make decorations and art, to dance, and to play ball games. However, on that day in 1492, the era of their isolation for the last three thousand years came to an end.

The Taínos had a rich culture, full of music, dance, sports, and art. This Taíno carving of a mythic bird was probably created sometime in the 15th century.

A Meeting of Strangers

Slowly, the boats crowded with the sunburned, bearded men pulled through the surf and scraped the bottom of the sandy white beach. The morning sun blazed overhead, and from the forest, flocks of parrots screamed and called. Giant, brilliant green trees and vines lined the beach. There were flowers everywhere, and tiny bee hummingbirds—the smallest birds in the world—were busy sucking up sweet nectar as they flew from blossom to blossom.

On the shore, small groups of Taínos had gathered, staring in amazement at beings such as they had never seen in their lives. Columbus stepped out of the first boat, dogged by his secretary who stood with quill and parchment poised, ready to record the admiral's historic words. Solemnly, Columbus decreed that he hereby claimed possession of the lands on which they now stood in the name of his masters, King Ferdinand and Queen Isabella of Spain. The secretary scribbled. Columbus and his men knelt

This 19th-century lithograph depicts Columbus and his men on the shore of the island, greeting the Taínos.

in the sand and offered a prayer to God for delivering them safely across the ocean to the Indies. They rose to their feet, sweating in the powerful tropical sun. Of course, the Taínos did not understand the significance of this act, but for explorers of that era, it was the acceptable and binding procedure for claiming land for their country.

Now that Columbus had claimed the land, he began looking it over as its new governor. The people, he noted to himself, were quite striking. They had the brown skin of the islanders he had seen in the Canaries and Azores, and straight hair that was different from that of the African slaves in Europe. They wore nothing except tiny **loincloths** and many went naked. All wore elaborate body paint in white, black, and red. On their faces, backs, and chests were painted intricate circles, parallel lines, geometric shapes, and pictures of animals. Their hair was long over their foreheads and down their backs. The men before him were tall, young, and looked strong and fit. They had no bulging bellies, Columbus thought, and had straight, muscled legs. They were also untouched by the disfiguring **smallpox** scars that marked almost every adult European. Most importantly, they carried no iron weapons. A few had long spears tipped with bone points. They were hardly a match for the armory carried by the Europeans.

> *The people, he noted to himself, were quite striking.*

The Taínos stared, too. They had never seen ships so big or men so strange. The only people they had known were other islanders like themselves, who came in canoes to trade and barter. The other islanders had always come in peace, except for one rather warlike group to the south with whom they sometimes fought.

The strangers seemed friendly enough. They gestured and held out trade goods—wonderful items the islanders had never seen before. Everyone was smiling. The men ran to tell others and get their own goods to trade.

The morning sun rose to its highest point, and the heat grew more intense. The officers were sweating in their woolen finery that covered them from neck to foot and down to their wrists. The islanders indicated that Columbus and his men should go with them to their village. Columbus was eager to see where these people lived. He must find out where the Khan was and if there was gold in the vicinity.

Visiting the Taíno Village

When they reached the village, the Europeans found that these people lived in huts that were then organized in circles around a large empty space. This space was used for meetings, ball games, and dances. The round huts were quite large. They were built of sturdy wooden poles set very close together and interwoven with dried grasses. The roofs were peaked to shed the rain, thatched with branches and vines, and then topped with a layer of waterproof palm leaves. Inside, the people hung bundles of sweet-smelling grasses to scent the air. They decorated the walls with thin strips of white bark twisted into elaborate patterns. Every person had his or her personal hammock for sleeping, woven from cotton and grasses.

This reproduction of a Taíno hut like the ones Columbus saw is located at Guanahani Landfall Park in San Salvador, Bahamas.

The Europeans admired these quarters, especially the comfortable hammocks. The clean, sweet-smelling houses with fresh breezes blowing through must have looked very appealing after the smelly conditions of the ships.

As they settled into the gathering space in the middle of the huts, the Taíno *cacique*, or chief, came forward to greet them. Each village had one of these *caciques*, who governed the people with the help of a small group of

Columbus had never seen sweet potatoes before. He thought they tasted like chestnuts.

elders. Columbus and his men were offered water and sweet potatoes, a root they had never seen before. There were no potatoes in Europe or Asia. Columbus thought the strange new food tasted like chestnuts. The entire village crowded around the visitors, fascinated by their sunburned, hairy appearance and bizarre clothing. Through signs and a few words, the islanders told the visitors that their island was called *Guanahani*.

To Columbus and his officers, the Taínos and their surroundings must have seemed primitive indeed. Theirs was a world of grass, reeds, water, cotton, and wood. They had no metal at all and very little stone. After the mighty palaces and cathedrals of Spain, the Taínos' huts must have seemed as flimsy as twigs snapping in the wind. Columbus had no idea—in fact, he would never really know—that he was looking at a culture that had not only lived but had also thrived without war, strife, or disease for thousands of years.

A Culture of Abundance

Almost all of the Taínos' success was due to their ingenious method of farming, which provided them with plenty of food without depleting the soil of its nutrients. Their staple crop was a root called *manioc*, also known as yucca or cassava. The Taínos also grew sweet potatoes, squashes, and beans. They planted the crops in fields of little hills of dirt called *conucos*. The crop was then cultivated with hand hoes and pointed sticks. This delicate system disturbed only the small area needed to grow each seedling, so the topsoil did not erode away.

The Taínos didn't spend all their time in the fields though. They were sophisticated fishermen, as well. The Europeans especially admired their huge one-piece canoes burned and shaped out of silk-cotton trees. The biggest of these could carry more than one hundred and fifty people. The Taínos had developed techniques to capture huge sea turtles from canoes. They even hunted manatees, enormous sea mammals that can weigh as much as two thousand pounds, from these canoes. They also created enclosed areas in the surf using reeds in which they kept thousands of live fish and turtles.

An American engraving, c. 1892, depicts the Taínos and their swift canoes.

Trading with the Native People

Columbus was very pleased with what he saw around him. True, there was no sign of the Grand Khan, but that was because they had surely reached an outlying island of China, he thought. The people would pose no problem in his quest. They were as gentle and friendly as children—in fact, they were remarkable in their openness and peaceful behavior. Fifty of them could be subdued by one of his men! Amazingly, they seemed to have no concept of the value of the parrots, javelins, and balls of cotton thread they were eager to trade. This situation could be used to a distinct advantage, Columbus thought, and he ordered his crew to hold back the bits of broken glass and rusted barrel hoops they were offering in return so that the islanders would think these worthless bits were of great value.

In this painting, created sometime between 1850 and 1900, Columbus's men trade with the Taínos while the captain himself addresses the crowd.

Bigger plans than trading for parrots were stirring in Columbus's mind. They must get started on their two missions: finding massive amounts of gold, spices, and jewels and making contact with the Grand Khan. Many of the islanders wore lovely gold jewelry crafted as nose rings. They indicated to Columbus that the gold had come from an island to the south. He would certainly visit there next, Columbus thought. That must be where the massive gold mines were located.

Columbus also realized there were commodities right here in front of him. These islanders were fit, strong, gentle, and naïve— they would make perfect slaves. Because they wore no clothes and had no iron, Columbus considered them heathens. It would be so easy to capture and disarm them and ship them back to Europe. They would turn a tidy profit when sold. Of course, Queen Isabella did not like slavery, but she might make an exception for such a value as this.

Columbus was happy but could not linger. The Grand Khan was waiting just around the corner. After two days of trading with the islanders, Columbus prepared to leave. He had realized, though, that if he were to find the Khan and gold, he must be able to communicate with the Taínos through more

Columbus was happy but could not linger. The Grand Khan was waiting just around the corner.

than signs. The solution, in his mind, was simple: He ordered his men to kidnap several Taínos and take them onboard the ships. They would be held as captives and taught Spanish so they could serve as the crew's interpreters on other islands. The crew secured their traded goods and prisoners and pulled up their anchors.

CHAPTER 8

Searching for the Khan

It was to create this impression [of goodwill] that I had set [the Taíno] free and gave him presents.

For two weeks, the *Niña*, *Pinta*, and *Santa Maria* sailed in and around the islands of the Bahamas. Everywhere they met friendly Taínos who swam or paddled canoes out to the ships to trade with the men. They amazed Columbus with their speed and agility.

Capturing the Taínos

Columbus was not content with the cotton and spears the natives would offer for trading. He wanted live captives to show Ferdinand and Isabella when he returned to Spain. Columbus's men regularly kidnapped some of the Taínos and held them on the ships as prisoners to take back across the ocean with them.

> *Columbus's men regularly kidnapped some of the Taínos and held them on the ships as prisoners . . .*

Although the Taínos were willing traders, they were not willing captives, and they would frequently try to escape. In his journal, Columbus described one incident in which some Taínos paddled a canoe alongside the ship on which two of their people were being held. One of the captives saw the canoe and jumped overboard into it. The canoe started moving away and the other captive leapt into the ocean and swam behind it. The Spaniards

gave chase but the Taínos beat them to the shore and ran to hide in the forest.

Columbus knew that the escaped Taínos would tell others that they had been kidnapped and forced to remain on the ship. He wanted captives, but he didn't want people to start hiding from him and his men. Columbus was already thinking of a second expedition, and he wanted the Taínos to remain peaceful and friendly when they came back. Columbus devised a scheme.

The next Taíno to approach the ship was a man in a canoe who wanted to trade for a ball of cotton. The man wouldn't board the ship, though. Perhaps he had heard about others being captured. So, some of the crew jumped into his canoe and grabbed him. They forced him onto the ship. Once he was aboard, Columbus gave him some green glass beads, one of the sailor's red caps, and two "hawk's bells"—little bells that are hung from the feet of falcons used for hunting. Then Columbus ordered the man released. "It was to create this impression [of goodwill] that I had set [the Taíno] free and gave him presents," Columbus later wrote in his journal. "I was anxious that they should think well of us so they may not be unfriendly when your Majesties send a second expedition here."

The falcon in this photograph is wearing bells on its feet. Columbus used gifts like falcon's bells to gain favor with the Taínos.

Arriving in Cuba

Near the end of October, the crew encountered a large landmass that is known today as Cuba. Finally, Columbus thought. This must be China, the home of the Grand Khan. Moreover, the people he found on this land wore much more gold than the others they had encountered. They had heavy gold bracelets and anklets—sure signs, Columbus assumed, that the gold mines of China were just over the hills.

Until now, Columbus had been very careful to observe all of the traditional rules of medieval European **diplomacy**. He had displayed the royal flag—the standard—of Ferdinand and Isabella when he first came ashore. The secretary had recorded his official speech that laid claim to the islands. Now they were ready to find the Khan's palace and inform him of their arrival. In keeping with tradition, an **emissary** team had to be assembled. The team would introduce itself to the Khan and offer him gifts in order to smooth the way for Columbus later.

This woodcut depicts Columbus and his men arriving in Cuba. The native chief greets them as men, women, and children look on.

Luis de Torres, the interpreter who spoke Arabic, was to head the emissary team and take with him a letter from Ferdinand and Isabella and a royal gift from the monarchs to the Khan. De Torres was also to bring the ship's passport, which was its identification document. The expedition set off immediately into the Cuban interior.

Columbus waited impatiently for their return. Meanwhile, he explored the island. He believed the forests were full of aloe, mastic, and spices—all valuable products in Europe. He ordered the ships packed full of wood, bushes, leaves, and berries, but what he didn't know was that the loads were worthless—he had actually misidentified all of the plants.

After about a week, the emissaries returned from the interior. Eagerly, Columbus questioned them. Did they find the Khan? What was his palace like? Did he receive them? Far from it, de Torres told his admiral. In fact, they had not found the Khan at all nor any palaces nor any riches. They had only found more of what they had already seen: villages of grass huts filled with islanders curious about the travelers but certainly no more laden with gold and jewels than the ones they had already met.

Where was the Khan, then? Where were the massive cities and giant ships of which Marco Polo had written? Wherever he was, it certainly wasn't on this island. No matter, Columbus thought. He was probably on the next island. It was time to move on.

Where Is the Gold?

Sailing along the Cuban coast, the crew soon encountered the coast of what is known today as Haiti. These islanders seemed more sophisticated to Columbus than the other ones they had previously encountered, and they had a little more gold.

A woodcut of a 1572 sketch shows various fruit trees of Hispaniola.

A cacique showed Columbus a piece of gold that was as big as a man's hand. The people indicated that there were mountains in the interior of this land. This was probably Japan, Columbus thought. Marco Polo had said that Japan had mountains. However, the island needed a new name, now that it had a new governor. The landscape reminded Columbus strongly of his beloved Spain and so the new island was christened "Hispaniola." Today, the island of Hispaniola is divided between the countries of Haiti and the Dominican Republic.

By now, it was the month of December. The weather on the islands had turned colder and stormy. Columbus's thoughts turned to the ocean crossing ahead of him. If they wanted to make it back to Europe this year, they must leave soon or risk a wintry month on the high seas. Columbus trembled a little when he thought of his reception with the monarchs.

He had promised them gold and jewels, and he had exactly none of these things, nor had he seen the Khan or any of his empire. He did have three ships full of spices—or what he thought were spices—as well as several Taíno captives, but this was not enough. The tiniest inkling that he might not actually be in the Indies wavered in Columbus's mind, but he quickly squashed it. He said he was going to find the Indies, he had found land where he said he would; therefore, this *must* be the Indies. He comforted himself with thoughts of how many slaves he could export later or keep here and force to work the mines and fields that he would soon establish.

Columbus sent out the word that the crew was to assemble on the coast of Hispaniola and make the ships ready to sail. Everything had to be inspected, repaired, sewn up, and stowed away. The men worked for days, scurrying on the decks of the massive ships like ants.

Shipwrecked!

On Christmas Eve, December 24, 1492, everything was ready. They would set out early in the morning. Everyone had gone to sleep, including Columbus. On the *Santa Maria*, only one ship's boy was left at the tiller—the bar used to help steer the ship. The night air hung thick and heavy, broken only by the gentle splashing of the waves against the ships' hulls. A thousand stars vaulted overhead.

The ship's boy nodded off and woke with a jerk, then fell asleep again. The tiller slipped gently from his loosening grasp. With a steady scrape, the current carried the flagship straight into

The *Santa Maria* is shown wrecked on the coral reef of Hispaniola in this hand-colored engraving.

shallow coral reef. It creaked and groaned against the coral and then shuddered and stopped, tilted at a crazy angle. The reefs had torn up the ship's bottom, ripping holes into it. The *Santa Maria* was wrecked.

After inspecting the damage, Columbus realized the ship could never be repaired well enough to make the journey back across the ocean. He would have to think of another plan. There was no way all of the men could fit on just the two ships. However, the natives were as friendly and peaceful as always, the island had plenty of food and water, and there was the need to find gold.

With that last thought of gold, the admiral made his decision. He ordered the ship's storage unloaded and the ship stripped of nails and timbers. In only a few short days, the sailors built a **garrison** on land, which Columbus named *La Navidad*, "Christmas," for the date on which the accident happened. He planned to sail back to Spain on the *Niña* and the *Pinta*, and he ordered thirty-nine men to stay behind at La Navidad with food, wine, tools, weapons—and most importantly, orders to find or trade for gold and have it waiting when he returned.

On the day of their departure, Columbus's spirits rose as the *Pinta* and the *Niña* pulled out of the bay, sails billowing. This time, they knew where they were going—home!

This woodcut showing the garrison La Navidad, built from the wreck of the *Santa Maria*, is from a 1493 illustrated edition of Columbus's letters.

How Columbus Navigated

Sailing a ship in the fifteenth century was not an easy job. By far the hardest part was navigation—directing a ship against the currents and waves until it reached the desired destination. Mariners in Columbus's time understood the ideas of latitude and longitude—the trouble was finding an accurate way to measure them. The medieval sailors had none of the devices sailors use today to help them: radios, radar, or global positioning devices.

To find latitude, sailors often used a tool called an astrolabe. This device measured the height and angle of the sun by directing a beam of sunlight through pinholes. They also used a magnetic compass to determine their direction. To measure the speed of their ships, sailors would toss an object, usually a knotted rope or a piece of wood, into the sea from the front of the ship. They would then measure on an hourglass how long it took the object to pass by the side of the ship. As you can imagine, except for the compass, none of these methods were very good. The astrolabe was notoriously hard to use accurately when standing on the deck of a pitching, bobbing ship. The floating object method gave only a rough estimate of actual speed. As a result, ships traveling to new places frequently misreported the distances or locations.

Medieval sailors used an astrolabe like this one to measure the angle of the sun.

Hourglasses like the one depicted here and knotted pieces of rope were used to calculate how fast a ship was traveling.

CHAPTER 9

The Triumphant Return

*Everyone in the city and court came out to
meet him.*

—*Fernando Columbus*

Standing on the deck, Columbus and his crew watched
the garrison recede in the distance, leaving them alone
again with the endless water they knew so
well. The seabirds soared over their heads,
and waves ran and broke into foam at the
bow of the ships.

Once more, Columbus's tremendous
self-confidence rose to his aid. The
monarchs would surely be thrilled that
he had found land exactly where he
said he would—and with so many
excellent new subjects. They were
all heathens, too. Isabella especially
was very keen on converting
heathens, and here he had
found her islands full. He
had the Taíno captives in
the hold to prove it.

Columbus was a proud,
confident man, even when
returning to Spain without
one of his ships.

True, the people he had met did not really seem like subjects of the Khan, but perhaps the islands he had found were just a little farther from the Indian mainland than he had originally thought. Either way, he would still get the rewards that were laid out in the Capitulations—everything he deserved.

Storm at Sea

After a few days, Columbus's calm, self-congratulatory mood was cut short. A terrible storm blew up one night. The men tied down the sails and closed the hatches, but after that, there was nothing to do but hang on and hope. For hours, the ships

On their voyage back to Spain, Columbus's ships were caught in a terrible storm like the one depicted in this oil painting.

pitched and rolled and men clung desperately to the ropes, vomiting at their feet. Black clouds rolled overhead and lightning flashed again and again, striking the sea.

Columbus knew the ocean, and he certainly had lived through bad storms at sea before. However, this one seemed especially fierce. The thought crossed his mind that they might die, which would be bad enough, but if they did—he concluded in terror—no one would ever know what he had done! The thought of the loss of his legacy must have terrified the admiral more than the loss of his life ever could. Quickly, he retreated to the rough shelter of his cabin and sat down. He must write immediately to the king and queen.

> *The thought of the loss of his legacy must have terrified the admiral more than the loss of his life ever could.*

Scratching at what must have been very damp parchment with his quill, Columbus wrote a letter describing everything he had done and seen. He begged the monarchs to award him his noble titles even after his death, so that his sons might carry them on. He made a copy of the letter to keep with him, and then placed the other copy in waxed cloth, placed it in a barrel sealed with wax, and tossed it overboard. Maybe someone would find it if he died.

Columbus need not have worried. The storm ended and all were alive, though the *Pinta* and the *Niña* had been separated. In another stroke of bad luck, the storm drove the *Niña* off course. Columbus made landfall in the harbor of the Azores Islands, the territory of the Portuguese, who were on the brink of war with Spain. Portuguese soldiers swarmed the ship as soon as it dropped anchor. Some of the crew were actually arrested and held until Columbus, furious and blustering, convinced the officials to release them or risk the wrath of the entire Spanish army.

Everything He Dreamed

This situation vastly improved once Columbus was safely home in Spain. He arrived in Palos harbor on March 15, 1493, and was received as a hero, just as he had hoped. The barrel with the letter he had written during the storm was never found, but Columbus had the copy still with him. It was rushed to printing, using the newly invented printing press. Eventually batches of the book would be reprinted fifty times.

Isabella and Ferdinand wasted no time in summoning Columbus to the court's current residence in Barcelona. "Everyone in the city and court came out to meet him," Fernando

This well-known 1893 chromolithograph by the Prang Educational Company shows a triumphant Columbus presenting Taíno captives to Isabella, Ferdinand, and their court.

Fernando Columbus

Fernando Columbus, whose name is also spelled Hernando or Ferdinand, was Christopher Columbus's son with Beatriz Enriquez de Arana. Although Fernando did not accompany his father on his first voyage, he played an important role in his father's life. A boy of only four when Columbus left on his first voyage, Fernando was left behind in Spain, but he was made a royal **page** after his father's return. During his life at the Spanish court, Fernando not only learned to read and write—skills that were rare in those days—but also became a scholar whose primary interest was books.

When he was fourteen, Fernando was permitted to accompany his now-famous father on his fourth and last voyage to the Americas. However, he was not an explorer at heart and soon returned to Spain, where he settled into a quiet life in Seville. After Columbus died, his son became the caretaker of his father's journals and papers. He used these, along with his own memories of the fourth voyage, to write a biography of his father in the late 1530s, titled *The Life of the Admiral Christopher Columbus.*

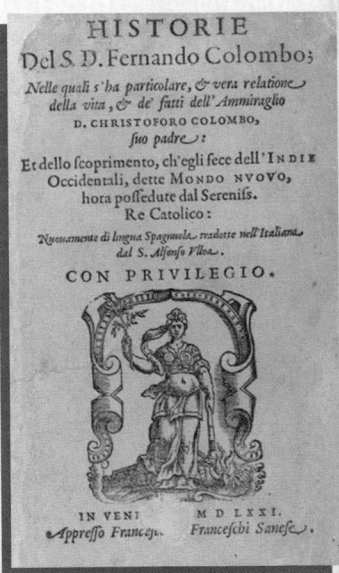

When he was an adult, Fernando Columbus wrote a biography of his famous father, the title page of which is shown here.

wrote in his father's biography. "[The] Catholic sovereigns, surrounded by their court, awaited him seated in all their greatness and majesty on a magnificent throne under a canopy of gold." All eyes were turned to Columbus as he mounted the steps to the thrones. He knelt triumphantly to kiss their outstretched hands, the spoils of his discovery behind him. It didn't matter that he hadn't found the Khan—yet—or brought home masses of gold. The promise of great riches was alive.

Columbus sat at the side of his king and queen and answered their questions about the journey. On the subject of whether or not Columbus had actually reached the Indies, though, the crown was neither accepting nor denying their adventurer's claim. They would wait and see, the monarchs murmured to each other. He was a hero though—there was no doubt about that. When finally the monarchs told Columbus he could go to his lodging house, the entire royal court accompanied him through the streets.

Those weeks in Barcelona would be the happiest of Columbus's entire life. He was honored with feasts and celebrations. He rode next to Ferdinand when the king paraded through the city. He was at the apex of his power: respected by the court, famous, titled, and with the promise of wealth at his fingertips. He had achieved his heart's desires—with more to come.

Best of all, Isabella and Ferdinand confirmed the Capitulations, the document they had all signed before the journey: They made Columbus governor of the lands he already found and any lands he might discover. He was to rule the people and have a ten percent share of any profits that came from establishing settlements.

A Columbian Legend

A legend is told about Columbus that has been proven untrue. Nonetheless, its attribution to Columbus illustrates his mythic status in Barcelona: Some noblemen were at a feast with the admiral. One noble was arguing that if Columbus had not made the journey across the ocean, someone else would have. Columbus took an egg and placed it on the table. He asked each man at the table to make the egg stand up on its end, using no props. When each man tried and failed, Columbus took his turn. He crushed one end of the egg and stood it up on its end, saying that once a deed is done, everyone knows how to do it, but the credit goes to him who thought of it first.

This undated illustration depicts Columbus showing off his egg trick to a group of noblemen.

Gold Above All

The captured Taínos were another matter. Isabella strongly disapproved of slavery. She was a Catholic and felt it was her duty to convert as many heathens as possible. Once the Taínos were converted, they could not be enslaved, according to the laws of Christianity. Only those who were beyond salvation could be enslaved. She was reluctant to authorize the import of slaves instead of gold—gold must be the first priority and slaves captured only if they were too devilish to be converted.

Plans went forward for a return trip to the Americas. Seventeen of the finest ships in the Spanish fleet were ordered fully stocked with food, wood, and weapons. They also brought seeds of wheat and barley. They would need to plant and grow their own food if they were to survive in their settlements. The word spread that the famous admiral's second voyage was soon to sail. Thousands of men thronged the docks. Everyone had heard the rumors of the incredible wealth to be had—gold just waiting to be discovered. Eventually, Columbus took on between twelve and fifteen hundred men, who would sail in a fleet of seventeen ships on September 17, 1493.

Plans went forward for a return trip to the Americas.

These passengers, who had beat out hundreds of others for the opportunity to sail under Columbus's command, had one goal in mind: wealth, either in the form of jewels, spices, humans, or gold. This intense desire coupled with the intoxication of conquest would soon combine into a potent, toxic brew.

"Indians"

When Columbus landed, he believed that he had reached the Indies—therefore, he thought, the people he met were "Indians." He was wrong, of course, but the name stuck. Even though more than five hundred years have passed since the voyage, the native people of the Americas are still frequently referred to as "Indians." However, some Native Americans prefer not to be labeled as such.

A 1728 etching depicts Columbus arriving again on the shores of Hispaniola and being greeted by Taínos. The explorer's belief that he was in India led him to label those he met "Indians."

CHAPTER 10

The Second Voyage

The Admiral and some of us landed and went to the site of the village. We found it completely burnt and the Spaniards' clothing lying on the grass.

—Diego Alvarez Chanca, physician on the second voyage

On November 27, 1493, after an uneventful crossing, the ships approached the reefs surrounding La Navidad. Night had already fallen though, and Columbus remembered what had happened to the *Santa Maria*. He would not try to pass through the reefs to shore in the dark. He ordered the anchors dropped. *Fffoom!* Bright flares arced into the night sky, signaling to those in the garrison that the ships had returned.

A Terrible Discovery

They waited. The shore remained dark. Finally, a canoe with a few Taínos bobbed up next to one of the ships. Through a few words, the Taínos indicated they wanted to see the admiral. Columbus allowed them onboard. Then he called one of the most valuable men in his crew to help. A Taíno whom the Spaniards

Finally, a canoe with a few Taínos bobbed up next to one of the ships.

called Diego Colon had been captured by Columbus on his first voyage. He made the trip back to Spain and was ordered to learn Spanish and become Columbus's

This colored woodcut depicts a Spaniard whipping a Native American woman, while other Taínos work and watch in the background. It might have been this cruel behavior that made the Taínos turn on the Spaniards.

interpreter. He made the second voyage with Columbus and was on the admiral's ship during that fateful night.

Colon stepped forward. "What was happening on shore?" he asked the Taínos. They launched into rapid speech. Diego listened carefully and then turned to the anxious captain. Bad news. There had been fighting. All of his men were dead.

The next morning, Columbus and his officers went ashore. The Taínos had told the truth: The garrison had been burned and destroyed, and the men's clothing lay scattered about. There were no survivors and none of the Europeans ever found out what really happened there. The Taínos had told Diego Colon that the men had fought among themselves, but later, some historians speculated that the crew had begun attacking the Taínos in order to seize their gold and had been kidnapping and raping the Taíno women. Perhaps the Taínos had fought back.

Columbus was eager to put the massacre behind him. He had no time to waste on dead men. He ordered a new colony established on a site seventy-five miles away from La Navidad, on the north coast of Hispaniola.

New Plants and Animals on Isabela

In early December 1493, the seventeen ships with more than a thousand men sailed along the coast to the new site. This colony was called *Isabela* after the admiral's beloved queen, and it was to serve as a base for the gold exploration and mining that

This medieval woodcut shows the settlement of Isabela, in the center of the picture. Isabela was one of Columbus's most important—and destructive—establishments.

Columbus was sure would take place as soon as they were settled. Over the next three years, it would become the center of the most horrific destruction and bloodshed the land had ever seen.

The men were straining to start searching for gold, but they needed food and shelter first. Columbus ordered them to build yet another garrison, unload the livestock, and begin breaking fields for crops. Most of the men considered these menial chores beneath them. After all, they had come here to find gold, not break their backs plowing.

The Spaniards had no idea, of course, but the plants, seeds, and animals they brought with them were going to change the entire landscape of the islands. Over the millennia, the continents of Europe and Asia had developed entirely separate **ecosystems** from North and South America—so different that the two cultures had never even seen the different plants and animals on each other's continents.

> . . . the plants, seeds, and animals they brought with them were going to change the entire landscape of the islands.

When the seventeen ships from Spain arrived on the shores of the Bahamas, they brought with them sugarcane, wheat, olives, oranges, lemons, pomegranates, dates, cucumbers, lettuce, melon, and grapes. These new species grew and spread, overwhelming the native plants that had existed on the continent for hundreds of thousands of years.

The ships had also brought animals: horses, cattle, sheep, goats, chickens, pigeons, and dogs. These animals were even more destructive to the islands than the plants. No large animals lived on the islands naturally, just rodents, birds, and turtles. The horses, cattle, and sheep consumed the native

Horses were unknown to the Americas before Columbus's time. They later spread to the mainland and became essential to the Plains Indians.

grasses and plants at an incredibly fast pace. They churned up the ground, and the soil began eroding at an alarming rate. The animals bred, and eventually many escaped from captivity. These animals had no natural predators at all, so their numbers grew enormously.

Struggle for Survival

Although the destruction of the island's delicate ecosystem was already in play, the effects of it would not be felt for a few more decades. Columbus now had more immediate problems. Before anyone could get started on wide-scale gold hunting, the

Before anyone could get started on wide-scale gold hunting, the men began to fall sick.

A Historical Trade

Though they had no idea at the time, the Europeans and the Taínos traded two things that would go on to shape entire cultures for the remainder of history: tobacco and the horse. The Europeans were utterly befuddled when they saw the natives smoking little bundles of dried leaves. No one had ever heard of lighting leaves and inhaling the smoke before. Soon though, the habit caught on among the sailors, and they brought some of the dried leaves back to Europe where others soon took up the pastime—and the first European nicotine addicts were soon created.

The settlers made their own contributions to North and South America. One of the most influential was the horse. The animal was native to Europe and Asia. Nothing like it had ever set foot on the islands

Tobacco leaves are shown here drying on a rack. Columbus's sailors went back to Spain smoking little bundles of these dried leaves. Europeans had never seen tobacco, but quickly became addicted to it.

or mainland of the American continents before 1493. Inevitably, some horses escaped and bred in the wild. Their numbers grew until the Americas were eventually home to thousands of herds moving through the grasslands of the continents. Horses would later transform entire Native American cultures when they were adapted for hunting.

men began to fall sick. Historians have speculated on what could have caused this, since the Taínos had lived for centuries on the island untouched by major illness. Some of the sickness may have been caused by the poor location Columbus chose for Isabela; the land was low and swampy, with swarms of mosquitoes and a poor, dirty water source. Most likely, the men were suffering not from one specific disease but from general exhaustion and poor nutrition.

The food crops also were not growing well. The Europeans had plowed large fields with teams of oxen and planted their crops as they were accustomed to doing, never considering the difference in the temperature, moisture level, and soil quality of the islands. The crops withered and died in the European-style fields while the cassava, corn, and yams in the Taínos' dirt-hill fields grew tall and bountiful. Already weakened by sickness, the settlers began to suffer from malnutrition on the island.

The food crops also were not growing well.

Nonetheless, no one was deterred from the ever-present search for wealth. Columbus organized every man who was able to walk into expeditions to be sent into the heart of the island to look for gold veins. Meanwhile, since the settlers had no food from their own crops, they regularly ordered the Taínos to supply them with cassava and yams. Until this point, the Taínos had generally thought of the Europeans as guests. Their culture was unusually open and friendly, and they were used to sharing whatever they had with others. However, a strain began to appear as the natives felt the pressure of hundreds of extra people to feed.

The Taínos endured terrible destruction by the Spaniards. In this woodcut, Spaniards on horseback burn a Taíno village and murder the people.

The Start of Enslavement

The Europeans needed food and shelter to sustain them while they searched for gold. All of this would take tremendous work—work that they were not willing to do. Why should they? The Taínos were right in front of them—they would make ideal slaves. The Spaniards were already used to enslaving people they encountered in their explorations, and the Taínos were no different—they had no weapons and were friendly and peaceful.

The Europeans began capturing and subduing Taínos, not just to take back to Spain, but to use as slaves right there in Isabela—to farm fields, cook, and act as servants. It wasn't hard to take captives and order them to work—the Europeans had chains and ropes with them. They also had swords and daggers and if the natives refused to work or obey orders, they were threatened or even killed.

Meanwhile, the expeditions kept returning empty-handed, infuriating Columbus and his officers. They were only finding little bits of gold that had washed down from the mountains and were sprinkled in riverbeds. There were no enormous lodes of gold at all.

Columbus was determined to profit, though, until the gold veins were found. If his men could not find the gold themselves, then the Taínos would have to find it for them. He imposed the gold tribute system. It was very simple: Every adult had to supply a certain quota of gold dust on a regular schedule. If they did, they were given a token to wear around their necks. If they didn't, they had a hand chopped off.

This woodcut depicts native people searching for gold under the gold tribute system, while Spanish colonists watch in the background.

Widespread Massacre

The implementation of the gold tribute system marked the beginning of the end for the Taínos. They refused to simply give up their lives for these strangers. Rebellions began and were brutally subdued. Anyone who was insubordinate was killed. In addition, the Europeans wanted the land for themselves, and the Taínos were in the way. If the natives weren't searching for gold or acting as servants, they were killed by sword or by hanging. If they showed the slightest sign of rebellion, they were killed. Brutal torture also was common and widespread. Within eighteen years, ninety-eight percent of the Taíno population would be dead. Those years were filled with violence and brutality.

In this engraving, c. 1590, Taínos are massacred by Spanish colonists. The Europeans inflicted wide-scale murder on the local population.

The Taínos fought back the best that they could, but they never had a chance. Their culture was almost entirely nonviolent. They had never even had the need to invent sophisticated weapons. Their agriculture, fishing, dance, and sports were highly developed, but their weapons were primitive. Their bows and clubs were no match for the Spaniards' swords, knives, armor, and attack dogs. Entire villages disappeared in hours, as dead bodies covered the ground and the huts were burned to ashes. Taínos began committing suicide in massive numbers, so desperate was their situation. They even began killing their children to keep them from torture by the Spaniards.

The Taínos fought back the best that they could, but they never had a chance.

From a modern view, this sort of slaughter is always hard to understand. The men who did these things were drunk on power and greed. In their new settlement, there were no laws to keep them under control. In addition, all of this violence and bloodshed was commonplace in the European culture of the fifteenth and sixteenth centuries. Everyone was used to the sight of public executions and torture, which were considered great entertainment for people. Violent street crime, murders, and robberies were everywhere in Europe. The **Spanish Inquisition**, with its gruesome torture and executions, was ongoing. Medieval Europeans did not have the same regard for human life as the gentle Taínos.

Sunk in a Quagmire

The food supply continued to decline as the Europeans failed to produce crops. They had come to be rich landowners, not toil like peasants. They insisted the Taínos feed them from their

Columbus, depicted here in an 1815 lithograph, knew his settlements were having trouble, and he left the Isabela settlement under his brother Diego's command in April 1494.

dwindling stores of cassava and yams. The natives could no longer work their own fields since the population was either dead or searching for gold.

Columbus was fed up with the settlement. Nothing was going as he planned, and the men still had not found enough gold to speak of. In April 1494, he left the settlement in the command of his little brother Diego and set out with a crew to explore Hispaniola's southern coast.

Along the way, the crew began to murmur that this land was not actually the Indies and that the great admiral was wrong.

If they began doubting him, he worried they might also stop seeing him as the final and ultimate authority in all areas.

Columbus had insisted to his men all along that these lands *were* the Indies. If they began doubting him, he worried they might also stop seeing him as the final and ultimate authority in all areas. They might get ideas of their own and leave him. Fearing the loss of his authority, Columbus drew up an oath stating these lands were the Indies without a question. He forced the men to sign it.

When Columbus returned to the Isabela settlement in September, he found the place in worse condition than when he had left. Without the promised easy riches, oppressed by the tropical heat, and without adequate food or water, the Spaniards had grown more and more discontent. Rivalries grew and the men split into different groups that fought each other. Diego had been unable to stop the infighting or end the regular Taíno rebellions as the natives struggled to hold on to the shards of their culture. The Spaniards were starving, and the natives, forced to provide for the settlers and themselves, were starving as well.

The settlers began turning their resentment against their leaders. In an attempt to appease them, Columbus instituted the *encomienda* system. Each colonist was given a piece of land and a group of natives as his own to work for crops and profit.

> *The settlers began turning their resentment against their leaders.*

Now that Columbus and his men had made the journey to the Americas twice, the route from Spain was charted and some of Columbus's seventeen ships were occasionally traveling from the Americas to Spain and back again. With these ships, the settlers sent letters home complaining of the mismanagement of the colonies, constant sickness, and the lack of food. Ferdinand and Isabella heard these reports and were beginning to wonder what was happening over in the new settlements. They had yet to receive the ships of gold their governor had promised them.

Slaves Instead of Gold

Columbus realized that the situation in Isabela was critical. He removed his brother from command and because he had no gold, he attempted to please the monarchs by sending them the only thing of value he had—Taíno slaves. Columbus shipped five hundred of them across the ocean to be sold at a market in Seville. This was a poor substitute for gold as far as Isabella was concerned. The queen was generally against slavery; heathens should be converted, not enslaved, according to her beliefs. However, she received the shipment of slaves, albeit reluctantly. Unable to give her anything else of value, Columbus kept sending more and more.

Although Queen Isabella was very religious, she reluctantly accepted Columbus's shipments of slaves. In this portrait, labeled *Isabella the Catholic*, she holds a Bible and wears a cross around her neck.

The crown did agree, however, that any person taken prisoner during the course of war could be enslaved. This was highly agreeable to Columbus and his men. They provoked the Taínos purposely and then took prisoner anyone who fought back.

It was very clear to everyone, including Columbus himself, that he was far better at captaining ships on the sea than governing on shore. His men had long since lost their doglike admiration for their governor. To make matters worse, Columbus fell sick in 1495. His bladder pained him terribly, his eyes burned, his sight deteriorated, and he developed crippling arthritis in his spine and joints.

> *It was very clear to everyone, including Columbus himself, that he was far better at captaining ships on the sea than governing on shore.*

He had to get back to Europe—to seek help for his pain and to explain the pitiful situation in the colony to the monarchs. Maybe he could even organize a third voyage of exploration. Getting back to captaining would surely make him feel better. He put his brother Bartolomeo in charge of the colony in his absence. Columbus hoped that he would do a better job than Diego. With two tiny ships, Columbus set sail for Spain in March 1496. One can easily guess what his thoughts must have been during this journey home: What had happened to his great expedition? How could he restore himself to glory?

CHAPTER 11

The Third Voyage

[De Bobadilla] . . . with no further delay or inquiry . . . arrested the Admiral and his brother Don Diego, sending them aboard ships where he put them in chains . . .

—*Fernando Columbus*

The moment Columbus returned to Spain, the admiral immediately started pleading for more supplies to quiet his angry settlers across the ocean who were still unable to support themselves. He also asked for ships and provisions for a new voyage of exploration.

This time though, there were no smiling monarchs taking Columbus by hand and inviting him to sit next to them. Isabella and Ferdinand were embroiled in a new war that was occupying most of their time. They were not eager to divert their attention to the badgering governor who had still not provided them with the riches he had promised.

Underway with Six Ships

Columbus had to wait for a year and a half before the monarchs found time to order ships outfitted for a return trip westward across the Ocean Sea. News of the harsh conditions in the colonies, lack of food, and most of all, lack of gold had spread during Columbus's absence. He was provided with a far poorer fleet than the one gathered for the second voyage. Only six ships were ordered, and in order to find the crew required for the journey, the court was forced to issue a notice stating that all criminals volunteering for the journey would be excused from punishment.

He was provided with a far poorer fleet than the one gathered for the second voyage.

Upon reaching the islands, three of the ships went directly to Hispaniola with the desperately needed supplies for the colony. Columbus took the other three with him for a bit of exploring. The fleet headed south along the string of islands that is today the Lesser Antilles, just north of South America, stopping to rest or fish along the way. Columbus must have found some relief from his worries during this journey. The annoyance of managing the unruly colonists was behind him and in front of him the sea, the place where he belonged.

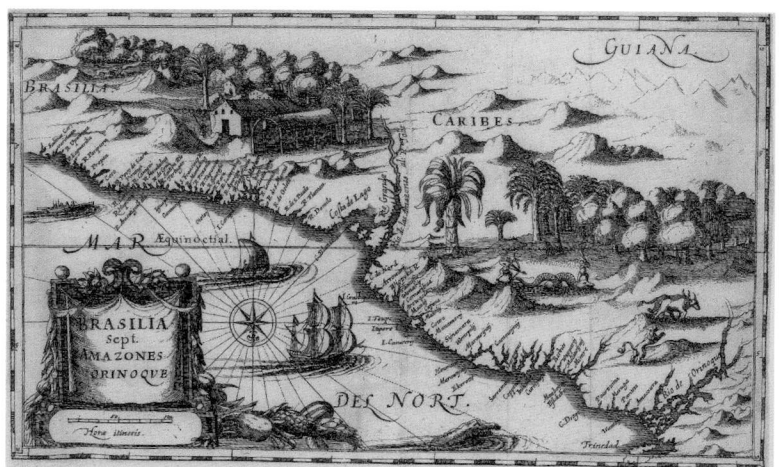

During his third voyage, Columbus discovered the coast of what we know now as South America. This medieval map of the northern coast of the continent shows the mouths of the Amazon and Orinoco Rivers.

After a few days, Columbus and his men found themselves sailing about in a large body of water. Today, this is known as the Gulf of Paria, on the coast of Venezuela, at the northeastern tip of South America. Columbus, though, only knew that there was a huge amount of fresh water flowing into this salty gulf. He assumed that he must be on the edge of a continent. The landmass had to be that big in order to support such large rivers. He was, in fact, correct, for he was at the delta of the Orinoco River, near what are today the nations of Trinidad and Tobago. On July 31, 1493, the crew landed on the shore of Trinidad and settled in for a few weeks of exploring.

Otro Mundo

For the first time, what Columbus believed he had discovered and what he truly had found were one and the same. He believed he had found a new continent, and he had—it was modern-day South America, but Columbus called it *Otro Mundo*, "another world." How could he reconcile this with his firm conviction that he was near the coast of the Indies? Columbus wondered.

This watercolor by Ernesto Casanova, c. 1880, depicts the explorer, and Columbus's rival, Vasco de Gama.

There was something else bothering him, too. Just before he left for the third voyage on May 30, 1498, he had heard the news that the explorer Vasco de Gama had sailed south around the Horn of Africa and had reached the shores of India, where he had met the rajah, or ruler of the land. No one doubted that de Gama had sailed to the Indies.

Then what was this massive landmass he had just found? What about the rest of the islands, Hispaniola and the others? Columbus pondered all of this. He could never accept the idea that he was not in the Indies—that he had been wrong all along. He decided that this continent must be a huge landmass *near the coast of the Indies*. He and Vasco de Gama had just reached the Indies by sailing in opposite directions and had met in the middle. Furthermore, the admiral decided that not only had he reached land, but he had in fact reached the one and only **Garden of Eden**.

Columbus believed he had found the Garden of Eden, depicted here in a 17th-century painting.

Columbus believed that the water in the gulf he had found was running *upward*, toward a point. In his mind, this point must be the mountain of Paradise that is mentioned in the Book of Genesis, in the Old Testament. Columbus called this "the nipple of the world," and reasoned that since he was near the Garden of Eden, then the four rivers that flowed into the gulf must also be the four rivers that are described in the Bible as flowing from Eden. He had found Paradise! Columbus immediately sat down and wrote a long letter to the monarchs to be sent on the next ship sailing to Spain, explaining all of this in detail.

This thinking must have seemed truly bizarre to the crown. Some of it can be explained by Columbus's inherent personality: All of his life, he saw only what he wanted to see. If something didn't fit into his plan, he just changed what he was seeing, rather than change the plan. Columbus was also in a great deal of pain during this time—almost constant pain. His joints bothered him terribly and his vision was very poor. He rarely slept and when he did, he was plagued by nightmares. The pain may have been affecting his thinking. Some historians have even speculated that the admiral was suffering from the beginning of mental illness.

The Threat of Rebellion

Columbus's spirit was greatly lifted by his discovery of Otro Mundo. He and the ships sailed directly back to Isabela, eager to spread the news about the discovered continent. His high spirits were ruined once he saw the state of the colony. Bartolomeo had proven just as inept at management as his brother Diego. The conditions were terrible; there was still no gold, no food, and sickness everywhere. A group of colonists had rebelled against the leadership of the Columbus brothers.

Destruction by Disease

The Taíno population was completely extinct within fifty years of the Europeans' first landfall. Some of this was due to murder and desperate suicides, as well as the declining birth rate, but disease was the most devastating factor in the demise of the Taíno people.

When Columbus and his Spanish ships arrived on the white beaches of the Americas, they unloaded a deadly cargo of dysentery, tuberculosis, and influenza in the form of the Spaniards. These diseases were common in Europe. Most adults contracted them and either died or survived with immunity. The sailors carried the germs in their bodies and spread them through everything they touched.

The native population had their own diseases that had existed among their people for centuries, but they had never encountered anything like this before. When there was an outbreak, the Taínos were completely overwhelmed. Within weeks, people began succumbing by the hundreds and then the thousands. At each island the Spaniards visited, they left behind a plague of death. At the height of the epidemic, Taínos lay dying on the ground in front of their huts. There were not enough living to bury the dead. Settlers wrote home about the unbearable stench of rotting bodies that filled the air.

This 19th-century engraving shows a group of Taínos on the beach. The native people were almost entirely extinguished by disease in the decades after Columbus's landing.

Led by the man Columbus had appointed as his chief justice, Francisco Roldán, the rebel group had moved to the other side of the island and had several hundred members. Bartolomeo and his men could not suppress them, though they had tried.

The situation was truly dire. Columbus immediately removed Bartolomeo from command, but it was too late. Columbus sent two ships filled with unhappy settlers back to Spain in early 1499. They carried word to Isabella and Ferdinand that their governor couldn't hold his colony together. The monarchs were fed up. They ordered Francisco de Bobadilla, a knight and trusted advisor, to sail to the colony. He was to investigate the situation and, if necessary, take control.

Returning Home in Chains

Before de Bobadilla could arrive, the event everyone had been waiting for occurred on Hispaniola. A mother lode of gold was discovered in December of 1499. Columbus was overjoyed. It was too late for him though. Roldán's rebels continued their struggle against Columbus and his brothers. The situation had deteriorated past the point of no return.

This couldn't have been more obvious than at the moment when de Bobadilla arrived at the settlement on Hispaniola in August 1500. Before his eyes, the corpses of seven Spaniards were hanging from gallows in the center of town. In his desperation, Columbus had ordered the men executed in a last-ditch effort to quell the rebellion.

That was enough for de Bobadilla. He ordered both Columbus and his two brothers stripped of command, arrested, shackled in chains, and sent back to Spain in disgrace—immediately.

Columbus is shown returning to Spain in chains and in despair in this 1905 illustration.

Columbus was furious. He was not a common criminal! He was the admiral of the Ocean Seas, governor of the Indies, discoverer of Paradise on Earth! What was *he* doing in chains? There was gold on Hispaniola! He had fulfilled everyone's dreams and now he was treated like a convict.

This was truly the lowest point in the life of the admiral. He was humiliated. When he arrived onshore, the law permitted Columbus to remove his shackles, but he refused. He wanted to make a statement about the abuses he had received at the hands of the crown by wearing his chains for all to see. To add to his fury, he had to wait six weeks before receiving an audience with the king and queen.

In this woodcut, a grand Nicolás de Ovando rides a white horse, surrounded by soldiers, as he surveys the land of Hispaniola as its newly appointed governor.

It was a sad and depressing meeting. Although Ferdinand and Isabella restored some of the rights granted to Columbus in the Capitulations—his share of the profits, the title of admiral—they did not reappoint him governor of Hispaniola. He had been deemed incompetent. A government employee named Nicolás de Ovando would take over in his place.

A Troubled Soul

Columbus's thoughts continued to grow in strange directions. He started dressing as a friar in simple gray robes, for reasons that have never been entirely clear. He may have been trying to atone for some of his sins. Perhaps it was a sign of his deepening sense of religion. He began working on a book that listed all the promises the Spanish crown had made to him over the years and the ways the crown had not honored these promises. Columbus called this his *Book of Privileges*, and he would continue writing it for the rest of his life.

He also began working on an even more bizarre text he called the *Book of Prophecies*. In this book, he insisted that all of his voyages had been divine missions directed by God. He wrote that he believed the world was coming to an end and that he, Columbus, was helping to bring this about. Day after day, Columbus remained at the court, working on his texts, wandering about in his friar's robes. Everyone wondered what to do with the troubled mariner.

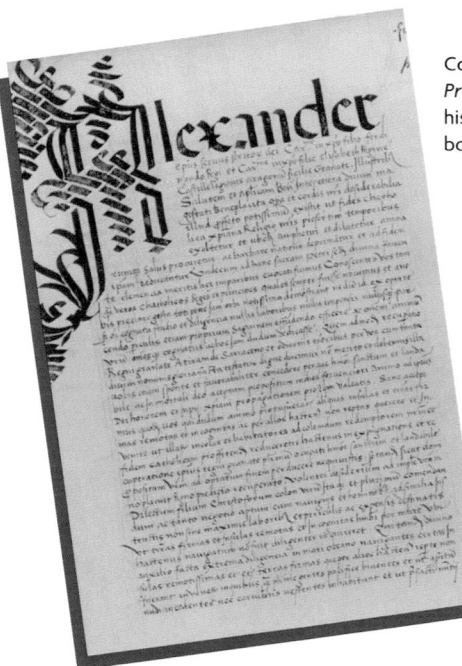

Columbus wrote his *Book of Privileges* during the rest of his life. A page of the actual book is shown here.

CHAPTER 12

The Last Voyage

Weep for me whoever has charity, truth, and justice!

Although Columbus had proven himself a terrible administrator, the king and queen still valued his skills at sea. They agreed to finance a fourth voyage because they still believed the Indies lay just west of the islands Columbus had found and north of the massive landmass Columbus had called Otro Mundo (South America). They wanted Columbus to search for a western **strait**—a passageway through these new lands that would get him to the Indies. Thus, four ships left Spain in 1502.

However, this trip was doomed from the beginning. It would go on to be a complete disaster. To start, the ships the crown gave to Columbus were all badly worm-eaten, which was a serious defect. Shipworms were tiny parasites that bored holes into wooden ships. They were capable of causing such widespread damage that if left unchecked, they could make boats sink. Columbus's worm problem only grew worse as the journey progressed across the Atlantic.

Banned from Hispaniola

To add to their troubles, the king and queen had given Columbus explicit orders not to land or go near the settlement when he arrived at the coast of Hispaniola. They may have been worried that he might try to take over some sort of leadership there again or that he would disturb the current governor. The admiral was outraged—

denied access to the land he discovered? However, Nicolás de Ovando, Columbus's replacement as governor, obeyed his monarchs. He ordered the admiral to drop anchor offshore rather than allow him into the colony.

Columbus, though, got his revenge—even if he hadn't planned on it. Before leaving, Columbus warned the governor that a hurricane would approach that night. He could tell the signs of an impending storm easily from a lifetime spent at sea. Because the governor did not trust the admiral, he not only ignored Columbus's warning but also ordered a fleet of twenty-eight ships loaded with gold to start on their journey to Spain that night.

Columbus and his men withstood the hurricane in their ships on the open sea. The Spanish fleet was not as lucky. All but three of the ships were lost, along with all their crew and cargo. One of the men who died was Francisco de Bobadilla, the knight who had arrested Columbus.

Stranded in Jamaica

From Hispaniola, the increasingly wormy, decrepit ships made their way around the coast of what is today Honduras, heading south toward modern-day Panama. Columbus was in excruciating pain. His eyes bled regularly, leaving him blind for long periods of time. He could barely sit or stand due to the pain in his joints. No one knows for sure what was ailing Columbus, but some medical historians believe it may have been a disease called Reiter's syndrome, which causes diarrhea and inflammation in the joints, eyes, and bladder.

> *Columbus was in excruciating pain. His eyes bled regularly, leaving him blind for long periods of time.*

In June 1503, the crew ran into storms near Panama. The worms had eaten the ships so badly that Columbus was forced to abandon two of them. He decided he had no recourse but to make his way back to Hispaniola—in spite of his banishment—to seek fresh men and supplies. However, the ships were too damaged. He got as far as Jamaica, only to be wrecked on the beaches.

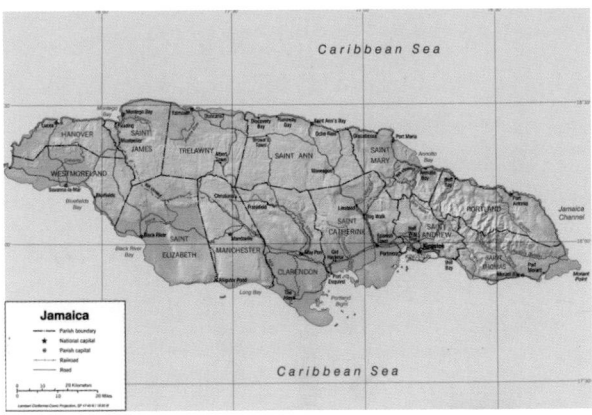

Columbus spent far more time than he intended on the island of Jamaica, shown here in a map from 2002.

Columbus was desperate. He and his men needed food and supplies, but the natives of the island were reluctant to help them. Columbus could tell from his **almanac** that an eclipse of the moon was about to occur. He told the natives that if they did not bring them food, fresh water, and supplies, the moon would be hidden forever. When the eclipse occurred as this strange man had predicted, the natives were so frightened that they supplied Columbus with what little they had.

The native population supported Columbus and the crew, who remained stranded in Jamaica for more than a year. Columbus sent some of his men to try to reach Hispaniola in canoes taken from the natives, but they had to turn back. Trying again, the crew finally reached Hispaniola on their second attempt. Once there, they found

The Indians Astonished at the Eclipse of the Moon foretold by Columbus.

Engraved for Drake's Voyages.

This 18th-century line engraving depicts Jamaican natives awed by the eclipse of the moon that was predicted by Columbus.

that though the new governor would allow the men to try to rescue Columbus from Jamaica, he did not want to waste one of the colony's ships on the attempt. The crew would have to charter a caravel from Spain—a process that took more than seven months. Finally, the ship—an incredibly old, worn-out ship—arrived in Hispaniola, and the men set out for Jamaica.

By the time he and his men were rescued on June 29, 1504, Columbus was beaten down. He was almost blind and in constant pain. He was exhausted and heartsick. While he waited in Jamaica, he had written a letter to his monarchs in which he spoke of the intense pain he was suffering. "Weep for me whoever has charity, truth, and justice!" he pleaded. There was nothing left for him in the lands he had discovered. On November 27, 1504, Columbus arrived in Spain, never to return to Hispaniola.

The Final Years

Upon his return to Spain, Columbus was basically ignored by the crown. He was a rich man from his share of the gold and slaves found in the early days of the colony, but he believed he had been cheated out of his rightful profits in recent years. His lifelong supporter, Queen Isabella, had died at the end of 1504, just as Columbus was returning to Spain. Without her, the king saw little reason to deal with the disgruntled old man before him.

This photomechanical print shows Christopher Columbus as an old man with gray hair.

Columbus spent his final years working on his *Book of Privileges*, in which he petitioned the crown over and over to restore the terms of the contract they had promised him— one-tenth of all the gold and other valuable goods found in the colonies, as well as the title of governor of those lands.

He descended into mystical religious thinking and began requesting funding for a brand-new sort of voyage: a Christian crusade to Jerusalem to rescue it from the Muslims. He followed the court from place to place during his last few years, still insisting on his privileges.

Finally, on May 20, 1506, at the age of 55, Christopher Columbus died at the court in Valladolid, Spain. No one really knows what killed him. Whatever the cause, the old mariner's death went mostly unnoticed. The official court registry did not even record his passing until ten days later. Columbus's body was laid in a crypt beneath the abbey of a monastery near the center of Valladolid.

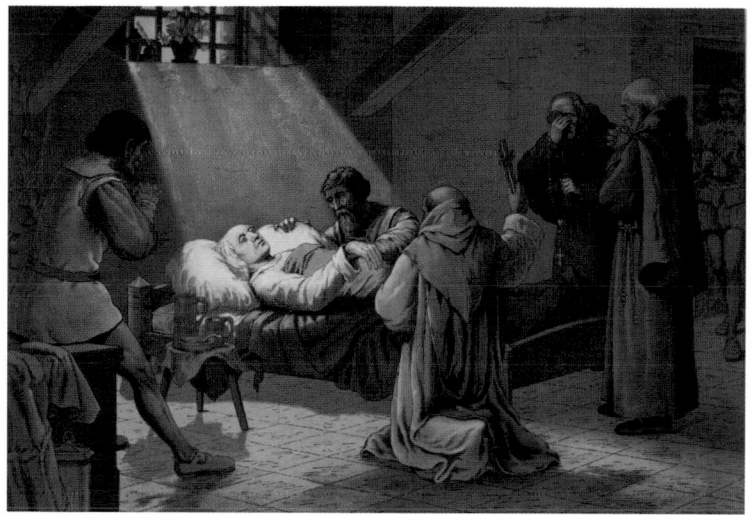

In this 1893 chromolithograph, Columbus is depicted on his deathbed. Unfortunately, he died an angry, unsatisfied man.

The Legacy of Columbus

In the years and decades following his death, much of the fame and glory Columbus desired was restored to him. He was heralded as the Father of the New World. Many people claimed to have known him personally, and sixteenth-century biographers scrambled to capture his story.

Throughout much of the rest of Western history, Columbus has been widely acknowledged as the first European to discover the islands of the Caribbean, Jamaica, Cuba, and the delta of the Orinoco River. Other explorers followed his westward routes and soon found the mainlands of North and South America and the civilizations that existed there. The colonies on the Caribbean islands grew and flourished and others were soon established on the coasts of the American continents. Columbus's exploration led this wave of settlement as countries, cities, villages, and

The Mystery of Columbus's Bones

For centuries, scholars have debated exactly where Columbus's remains lie. Three years after his death, his son Diego had his father's body removed from the crypt in Valladolid to a monastery in Seville. Ten years later, after Diego's death, his widow had both her husband and Columbus's bodies moved to a cathedral in Hispaniola (present-day Dominican Republic). Sometime during the eighteenth century, Spain dug up what they believed to be Columbus's remains and carried them from Hispaniola to Havana, Cuba. When Cuba became an independent country, the bones were moved once again, back to Seville.

Some scholars believe that in all of this moving, Columbus's remains were mixed up with those of his son Diego. Some Cuban historians have argued that the body was never transferred from Cuba at all and still remains in the cathedral in Havana.

In 2006, scientists confirmed that at least some of the bones resting inside Columbus's crypt in Seville were indeed those of the explorer. However, some of his bones may still remain in the cathedral in Havana. The Cuban authorities refuse to open the crypt to allow testing. Until they do, the rest of the mystery of Columbus's bones will never be solved.

For almost four centuries, the Santa Maria la Menor Cathedral in what is now the Dominican Republic held the bones of Columbus and his son Diego.

streets were named after him. In the United States, Columbus Day is a national holiday that is celebrated on the second Monday in October.

In more recent years, however, Native Americans of North and South America and the Caribbean islands have argued that Columbus did not actually "discover" anything. Hundreds of thousands of native people lived and thrived on the islands far before any European set foot there. How could Columbus "discover" a place so many people already called home? Moreover, many have pointed out that in celebrating Columbus, we are not considering the utter destruction of the Taíno culture and the eventual extinction of the native population from murder and disease.

Nevertheless, the man himself has been called glorious, brave, and a visionary. However, history shows that he was also destructive, cruel, greedy, and brutal. He was a man of many contradictions—a brilliant mariner and admiral on the ocean but a poor governor and leader on land; a courageous explorer who dared to follow his instincts but a cowardly rogue who resorted to murder and torture to obtain wealth. In spite of these contradictions—or perhaps, because of them—Columbus opened the routes to exploration and settlement of the Americas, helping to create the world we know today.

Columbus is remembered and memorialized all over the world. Though he is a controversial figure, no one denies that he influenced the course of history.

Glossary

almanac—a book with information about astronomy, including the positions of the sun, moon, and stars at various dates.

aloes—plants with spiky leaves containing a juice valued for its health properties.

apothecary—a medieval pharmacist who mixed and dispensed drugs.

becalmed—motionless due to lack of wind.

bow—the front of a ship.

Crusades—military expeditions by knights during the Middle Ages to take Jerusalem and the Holy Lands from the Muslims who possessed them.

diplomacy—the conduct of negotiations and other relations between governments or nations.

ecosystems—plants, animals, and other living organisms that function together as a system within a certain environment.

emissary—a representative sent on a mission.

entourage—a group of people who accompany an important person.

entrepreneur—a person who organizes or manages an enterprise, usually a risky one.

Garden of Eden—the beautiful paradise named in the Bible as the home of Adam and Eve.

garrison—a fortified military site.

Gregorian calendar—a solar calendar created in 1582 by Pope Gregory XIII as a corrected version of the Julian calendar.

heathen—a person who does not believe in the God of the Bible; an uncultured, nonreligious person.

Julian calendar—a solar calendar introduced by Julius Caesar in 46 BCE, eventually replaced by the Gregorian calendar.

loincloths—small pieces of cloth worn around the hips.

medieval—relating to the Middle Ages, a period of European history dating from about 500 CE to about 1500 CE.

mutiny—a rebellion of sailors against their superior officers.

navigate—to control the course of a boat or ship over a planned area.

page—in medieval times, a boy who lived at the royal court and was being trained to become a knight.

rigging—the system of ropes and chains that support the masts and sails of a ship.

smallpox—a contagious disease that leaves deep, disfiguring scars. During the Middle Ages, smallpox epidemics were frequent in Europe.

sovereignty—supreme power or authority.

Spanish Inquisition—an investigation started in 1478 by the king and queen of Spain to protect Catholicism in the region; it lasted until the early nineteenth century and was notable for the tortures and executions of the fifteenth and sixteenth centuries.

strait—a narrow passage of water through land that connects two larger bodies of water.

ward—a person placed under the care and protection of a guardian.

Bibliography

Books

Cohen, J. M., ed. *The Four Voyages of Christopher Columbus: Being His Own Log Book, Letters and Dispatches with Connecting Narrative Drawn From the Life of the Admiral by His Son Hernando Colon and Other Contemporary Historians*. New York: Penguin Books, 1969.

Colon, Fernando. *The Life of the Admiral Christopher Columbus by His Son Ferdinand*. Trans. Benjamin Keen. New Brunswick, NJ: Rutgers University Press, 1992.

Morison, Samuel Eliot. *Admiral of the Ocean Sea: A Life of Christopher Columbus*. Boston: Little, Brown, 1942.

Sale, Kirkpatrick. *The Conquest of Paradise: Christopher Columbus and the Columbian Legacy*. New York: Knopf, 1990.

Stannard, David E. *American Holocaust: Columbus and the Conquest of the New World*. New York: Oxford University Press, 1992.

Symcox, Geoffrey and Blair Sullivan. *Christopher Columbus and the Enterprise of the Indies: A Brief History with Documents*. New York: MacMillan, 2005.

Thornbrough, Emma Lou. *The World of Christopher Columbus: Imperial Spain, 1469–1598*. Acton, Mass.: Copley Publishing Group, 1997.

Wilford, John Noble. *The Mysterious History of Columbus*. New York: Random House, 1991.

Periodicals

Auster, Bruce B., "A Leaf from Leif," *U.S. News and World Report*, July 24, 2000.

Brown, David E., "What They Carried," *New York Times*, June 6, 1999.

Cohen, Bernard, "What Columbus Saw in 1492," *Scientific American*, December 1992.

Fernández-Armensto, F., "Columbus—Hero or Villain?" *History Today*, May 1992.

Holmgren, V. C., "The Unheralded Story of Columbus," *Sea Frontiers*, February 1992.

Hughes, R., "Just Who Was That Man?" *Time*, October 7, 1991.

Katz, William Loren, "Columbus and the American Holocaust," *New York Amsterdam News*, October 19, 2003.

Kolbert, Elizabeth, "The Lost Mariner," *New Yorker*, October 14, 2002.

Sarna, Jonathan B., "Columbus & the Jews," *Commentary*, November 1992.

Stannard, David E., "Genocide in the Americas," *The Nation*, October 19, 1992.

Source Notes

The following citations list the sources of quoted material in this book. The first and last few words of each quotation are cited and followed by their source. Complete information on referenced sources can be found in the Bibliography.

Abbreviations used:
FV—The Four Voyages of Christopher Columbus

Note: The Four Voyages of Christopher Columbus *by J. M. Cohen is a compilation of primary source documents written by Columbus himself, his son Fernando, and other biographers of the time. The words in quotation marks are not Cohen's, but are those of the people mentioned.*

LA—The Life of the Admiral
MHC—The Mysterious History of Columbus

INTRODUCTION: A Historic Voyage
   PAGE 1 *"The Admiral most seriously . . . carefully for land"*: FV, p. 53

CHAPTER 1: The Boy Cristoforo
   PAGE 2 *"Two things . . . his family"*: LA, p. 3

CHAPTER 2: The Seeds of an Idea
   PAGE 12 *"[Christopher] Columbus . . . left for Portugal"*: FV, p. 28

PROPERTY OF
DEL NORTE MIDDLE SCHOOL
DEL NORTE, CO 81132

Image Credits

© Ivy Close Images/Alamy: 31
© CORBIS: 2, 22
© Archivo Iconografico, S.A./CORBIS: 14, 36
© Bettmann/CORBIS: 4, 24, 43, 82
© Michelle Chaplow/CORBIS: 46
© Christie's Images/CORBIS: 32, 103
© Werner Forman/CORBISL 59
© Jeremy Horner/CORBIS: 28
© Dave G. Houser/Corbis: 62
© Hulton-Deutsch Collection/CORBIS: 18
© Danny Lehman/CORBIS: 116
© Adam Woolfitt/CORBIS: 68
© Monika Adamczyk/Dreamstime.com: 10
© Michael Cutri/Dreamstime.com: 50
© Rafal Fabrykiewicz/Dreamstime.com: 90
© Martin Garnham/Dreamstime.com: 117
© Stephen Sweet/Dreamstime.com: 58
© Michael Thompson/Dreamstime.com: 21
Getty Images: 45
The Granger Collection, New York: 7, 16, 17, 25, 41, 64, 74, 77, 94, 105, 113
© iStockphoto.com/"Christine Balderas": 75 (bottom)
© iStockphoto.com/"Mary Morgan": 89
© iStockphoto.com/"Mark Pruitt": 20
© iStockphoto.com/"Norbert Speicher": 75 (top)
© iStockphoto.com/"Clee Villasor": 51
© iStockphoto.com/"Yin Yang": 63
Library of Congress: 5, 12, 26, 33, 34, 35, 37, 38, 42, 47, 48, 53, 57, 60, 65, 76, 79, 80, 84, 96, 98, 101, 102, 107, 109, 112, 114, 115
© North Wind / North Wind Picture Archives: 15, 54, 56, 69, 71, 73, 86, 87, 92, 93, 108
Cover art: Stock Montage/Getty Images

About the Author

Emma Carlson Berne has written and edited more than a dozen books for children and young adults, including biographies of such diverse subjects as Laura Ingalls Wilder, William Shakespeare, the Hilton sisters, and Snoop Dogg. She lives in Cincinnati, Ohio.

Index